IMAGES
of America

CAMP CROWDER

ON THE COVER: The main gate for Camp Crowder during World War II was Lyon Gate, which was named in honor of Nathaniel Lyon—the first Union general to be killed in the Civil War. General Lyon died in the Battle of Wilson's Creek near Springfield, Missouri, on August 10, 1861. The guard shack pictured here no longer stands, but West Lyon Drive remains as a four-lane highway also known as Route D. (Courtesy of Missouri State Archives.)

IMAGES
of America

CAMP CROWDER

Jeremy P. Amick
Foreword by Charles Machon

ARCADIA
PUBLISHING

Copyright © 2019 by Jeremy P. Amick
ISBN 978-1-4671-0257-5

Published by Arcadia Publishing
Charleston, South Carolina

Library of Congress Control Number: 2018952324

For all general information, please contact Arcadia Publishing:
Telephone 843-853-2070
Fax 843-853-0044
E-mail sales@arcadiapublishing.com
For customer service and orders:
Toll-Free 1-888-313-2665

Visit us on the Internet at www.arcadiapublishing.com

I would like to dedicate this work to my friend and US Army veteran, the late Mort Walker. Through Camp Swampy in his Beetle Bailey comic strip, he has provided Camp Crowder with renewed life and an enduring legacy.

Contents

Foreword		6
Acknowledgments		7
Introduction		8
1.	Carved from the Wilderness	11
2.	Hustle and Bustle of Camp Life	33
3.	Leadership	61
4.	Entertainment, Celebrities, and Recreation	71
5.	Prisoners of War	79
6.	Memorabilia	87
7.	The Surrounding Communities	103
8.	Camp Crowder after World War II	113
Bibliography		127

Foreword

For the Missouri history lover, those who admire military history, or someone who appreciates World War II history, the establishment of Camp Crowder is an important aspect of our state's rich military legacy. As the director for the Museum of Missouri Military History, Camp Crowder has been an important focus of our preservation efforts and possesses a fascinating background—from its halcyon days as a training center for the US Army Signal Corps to its present-day use as a training site for the Missouri National Guard. As this book explains, the iconic Carl Reiner trained there during World War II and later embraced his days at Camp Crowder to create the character Rob Petrie (played by Dick Van Dyke) as a person who had trained there as well. Our museum's preservation efforts frequently turn to the late Mort Walker, who was stationed at Camp Crowder and whose *Beetle Bailey* comic strip was patterned after his time there. The military post also housed German prisoners of war during the war, leaving their mark in forgotten and tucked-away areas. Sections of this book also bring the reader to the present day by illustrating how the Missouri National Guard has transformed Crowder into a top-notch training facility not only utilized by the National Guard, but other branches of service as well.

—Charles Machon
Director, Museum of Missouri Military History

Acknowledgments

There are many historical societies, organizations, veterans, and Missouri National Guardsmen whose knowledge and resources have, through some means, contributed to this book. I must thank Tony Bamvakais and Brett Cooper for assisting me in the coordination of visits to the sections of Camp Crowder operated and maintained by the Missouri National Guard. Additionally, I must acknowledge the "boots on the ground" assistance offered by Jason Snyder and Tia Hicks, as they escorted me around post to photograph and research areas of Camp Crowder's history that have nearly been consumed by the passage of years. In addition, Charles Machon and Doug Sheley, with the Museum of Missouri Military History, were not only able to answer a number of questions I had about the camp's history but also provided several fascinating photographs to use in the book. Finally, a "tip of the hat" to all the efforts of the Missouri State Archives for preserving and offering for print scores of photographs from the glory days of Camp Crowder in World War II. Thank you everyone for your assistance in preserving the history of "Camp Swampy."

INTRODUCTION

Fort Leonard Wood has for decades been recognized as Missouri's US Army base. Carved from the wilderness of the rugged Ozarks, ground breaking for the fort occurred on December 3, 1940—a year prior to the United States' entry into World War II. The 61,000-acre military fort was completed in June 1941 with "nearly 1,600 buildings (constructed), comprising five million feet of floor space," wrote Dr. Larry Roberts in the summer 2008 issue of *Maneuver Support Magazine*. However, at the same time Fort Leonard Wood was nearing completion, a group of officers from the Seventh Corps Area investigated sites in Missouri for another Army base, where additional troops could be trained for the country's anticipated involvement in World War II.

"The desirability of the site depended upon such things as water supply, railroad facilities, topography, location of transcontinental highways and other military needs," wrote the late Don Mayes in a now rare souvenir booklet of Camp Crowder's construction published in 1942. He added, "Neosho was recommended and thus was the beginning of Camp Crowder."

Burns and McDonnell Engineering Company of Kansas City was awarded the contract to oversee construction of the camp, and on May 28, 1941, moved into a building in nearby Neosho to begin their work. For the next few months, the firm was busy surveying, mapping, and drawing up site plans for the proposed camp. "The War Department has designated a tentative camp site in the Neosho area but actual construction will not be started unless the army is expanded to about 2-1/2 million men," reported the *Moberly Monitor-Index* on June 20, 1941. The paper went on to explain that no land acquisitions had yet been made for the proposed camp.

Approval for the site was soon granted, the necessary land acquired, and the official groundbreaking ceremony held on the site on August 30, 1941. The site was officially named Camp Crowder on September 24, 1941, in honor of the late Maj. Gen. Enoch H. Crowder, a Missourian best known for drafting the Selective Service Act of 1917. Initially, it was anticipated the camp would sprawl across an impressive 66,500 acres; however, on November 7, 1941, the *Moberly Monitor-Index* reported that the War Department had disclosed plans to reduce the size of Camp Crowder "by about 11,000 acres on the eastern boundary" due to the proximity of homes and schools.

The reduction in acreage did not diminish the tempo of construction, and the first troops began to arrive at the camp on December 2, 1941. Less than three weeks later, a peak employment of 20,534 was reached at the site. One month later, as the calendar transitioned to January 2, 1942, a total of 81 buildings were ready for occupancy, and by January 29, this number rose to 352 usable buildings. Dedication ceremonies were held on April 12, 1942, and attended by a crowd of thousands. While speaking at the ceremony, Gov. Forrest Donnell recognized not only the role the camp would serve in training soldiers for combat, but also acknowledged those who toiled in its construction. "Patriotism is not confined to those who wear the uniform," said Donnell. "I take this opportunity to pay a word of tribute to all those who have engaged in the construction of this camp."

In February 1942, Camp Crowder became the second replacement training center for the Signal Corps—the branch of the Army that manages communications. In June 1942, the Midwestern Signal Corps School opened, and the camp became "the largest concentration of Signal Corps recruits . . . although it had been in operation less than four months," as noted in *The Signal Corps: The Test*. Kansas City native Mort Walker was stationed at Camp Crowder for several weeks during World War II, where he received the inspiration for what years later became "Camp Swampy" in his popular *Beetle Bailey* comic strip. Actor and writer Carl Reiner, creator of *The Dick Van Dyke Show*, also spent time at the camp during his wartime service.

In addition to the military training provided at the camp, it housed approximately 2,000 prisoners of war during World War II. When the war came to an end in late summer 1945, operations at the camp began to wind down and the site was eventually closed. Camp Crowder experienced a mild resurgence during the Korean War, and a portion of the property was used by the Air Force during the Cold War to test rocket engines, but much of the original property has since been deemed excess and sold off to private interests, including Crowder College and the Missouri Department of Conservation. The Missouri National Guard retained 4,358 acres of Camp Crowder for use as a training site. Now a fraction of its World War II size, the camp currently has a full-time staff of approximately a dozen employees—a sharp contrast to the more than 40,000 uniformed men and women it was home to at the height of war. Despite these changes, the camp provides a training home to the next generation of soldiers, who can still hear echoes of its storied past.

"Personally, I grew up in the area and I at no point in time heard what a significant role Crowder played during World War II," said Jason Snyder, a member of the Missouri National Guard who has served as base operations supervisor for the site. "The building foundation and some of the walls from an old German school from World War II are still standing on the south side of the camp and have kind of been hidden by time," he said, adding, "there is even German writing still visible on some of the walls." He concluded, "The German prisoners once held here are only a part of the site's rich legacy and it is certainly a privilege to be associated with something that has played such an important role in our state's military history."

One

CARVED FROM THE WILDERNESS

Camp Crowder was named in honor of Maj. Gen. Enoch H. Crowder, a native Missourian who graduated from the United States Military Academy at West Point in 1881. Although he would go on to complete 50 years of public service, Crowder has garnered his greatest recognition for the development, implementation, and administration of the military draft in World War I. (Courtesy of the Museum of Missouri Military History.)

Prior to settling on the name of Camp Crowder, the initial title for the Neosho project was Camp Cockrell—in recognition of Francis Marion Cockrell, who served as a Confederate general during the Civil War. In later years, Cockrell served as a US senator and was a candidate for the Democratic presidential nomination in 1904. (Courtesy of the Library of Congress.)

A small group of employees from Burns and McDonnell Engineering Company of Kansas City and US Army engineer staff arrived at Neosho on May 8, 1941, to secure working quarters for the construction of the site that would weeks later be designated Camp Crowder. Among those in this party were James C. Stewart, who is pictured in his office at Camp Crowder shortly after receiving a promotion to the rank of captain. (Courtesy of the Museum of Missouri Military History.)

On May 9, 1941, Burns and McDonnell was presented with the signed contract for surveying, mapping, preparing plans and, if approved, overseeing construction of the camp that would soon become Camp Crowder. Pictured is Chester A. Smith, who served as the resident director for Burns and McDonnell during the construction process. (Courtesy of the Museum of Missouri Military History.)

Employees of Burns and McDonnell moved into the Haas Building in Neosho beginning May 28, 1941, after signing a lease for the entire third floor of the former grocery building. Among the personnel who took part in the move was Claude K. Matthews, the company's chief engineer during the construction of the camp. (Courtesy of Burns and McDonnell.)

It was in late June 1941 that employees of Burns and McDonnell forwarded to the War Department in Washington, DC, their survey and plans for the new Army cantonment that was being planned near Neosho. The engineering firm was cofounded by Robert E. McDonnell, who passed away in 1960 and was laid to rest in Calvary Cemetery in Kansas City. (Courtesy of Burns and McDonnell.)

There were a number of attempts to hold ground-breaking ceremonies for the site that would become Camp Crowder, but the US Army, the Neosho Ad Club, civic groups, and the engineering and construction companies involved in the project could not agree on a date. It was finally agreed to hold the official ground breaking on August 30, 1941. Less than a year later, soldiers assigned to the post were able to purchase postcards such as this at the post exchange to send home to their loved ones. (Author's collection.)

Although the official ground breaking was held on August 30, 1941, the site would not officially be named for the late Maj. Gen. Enoch Crowder until September 24. Following the ground breaking, dozers and other heavy equipment began clearing roads and areas for the hundreds of buildings that would soon be erected. (Courtesy of the Museum of Missouri Military History.)

Assigned to the area engineers for the US Army at Camp Crowder, Capt. Fred L. Houston served as the assistant property and procurement officer during the construction process. He and his wife were living in nearby Neosho when she gave birth to their son George Brinkley Houston at the community's Sale-Bowman Hospital in January 1942. (Courtesy of the Museum of Missouri Military History.)

A native of Maryland, William Cover Smith is pictured in his office at Camp Crowder in early 1942, when he was the office manager and auditor representing Burns and McDonnell during the camp's construction. In later years, Smith was employed as an accountant. He passed away in 1963 at 62. (Courtesy of the Museum of Missouri Military History.)

Burns and McDonnell Engineering Company awarded contracts for the construction of the camp to McDonald Construction Company and the G.L. Tarleton Inc. Construction Company of St. Louis. Tom Knobel, who served as the general project superintendent for the camp's construction, is cutting pieces of his cake during a birthday celebration in early 1942. (Courtesy of the Museum of Missouri Military History.)

Lt. Lee B. Stoney, pictured in his office in January 1942 surrounded by blueprints of Camp Crowder, was one of the US Army officers brought in to serve as the operations officer for the area engineers while the camp was under construction. Prior to his transfer to Camp Crowder in December 1941, Stoney was assigned to Fort Smith, Arkansas, and previously served with the Army in Omaha, Nebraska. (Courtesy of the Museum of Missouri Military History.)

A young 2nd Lt. Wendall H. Benway is pictured in early 1942 while serving as expediting and assistant engineer officer with the US Army Engineers assigned to the camp. During this time, according to the February 5, 1942, *Cassville Republican*, word was received from the army engineer's office in Kansas City that troop facilities at both Camp Crowder and Camp Chaffee, Arkansas, would double in size. (Courtesy of the Museum of Missouri Military History.)

In the summer of 1941, 1st Lt. Stanley W. Nitzman was appointed an engineering officer to assist the construction quartermaster assigned to the project at Camp Crowder. Years later, Nitzman was employed as the chief of the Engineering and Construction Division of the Schenectady, New York, office of the US Atomic Energy Commission. (Courtesy of the Museum of Missouri Military History.)

During the camp's construction, Lt. Samuel T. Whitebread served as the area engineer representing the US Army. On December 12, 1941, the soldier was quoted in the *St. Louis Post-Dispatch* as stating the construction at Camp Crowder was 50 percent completed, with an employment level of 18,374. (Courtesy of the Museum of Missouri Military History.)

1st Lt. Victor Stefan Rauzi became the auditing and expediting officer for the US Army during the construction of Camp Crowder. He would later achieve the rank of lieutenant colonel and work full-time with the Wyoming Employment Security Commission. While on a two-week training exercise in Chicago with the Army Reserve, the 49-year-old Rauzi died unexpectedly on May 15, 1962. (Courtesy of the Museum of Missouri Military History.)

Harold C. Henning is pictured with his administrative assistant while employed as the purchasing agent for Burns and McDonnell during the early weeks of 1942. In 1962, Henning and his wife perished in an explosion at their home near Emporia, Kansas, believed to have been caused by an accumulation of gas fumes. (Courtesy of the Museum of Missouri Military History.)

Capt. Norman Vincent Gomes was called to active duty with the US Army in 1941 and served as post engineer for a prisoner of war camp in Scottsbluff, Nebraska. He later became the auditing captain during the construction of Camp Crowder and was later discharged from the Army at the rank of major in 1946. The veteran died September 12, 2005, and was laid to rest in Springfield National Cemetery. (Courtesy of the Museum of Missouri Military History.)

Robert Otis Beale is pictured in his office during the construction of Camp Crowder in late 1941. Beale was employed by the former St. Louis–San Francisco Railway, and during the construction of Camp Crowder served as depot agent overseeing many of the freight delivery operations. He passed away in 1973 and was laid to rest in Maple Park Cemetery in Aurora, Missouri. (Courtesy of the Museum of Missouri Military History.)

Specific site plans for the pending US Army cantonment were agreed upon and signed on August 1, 1941, and the government was granted permission to occupy the site seven days later. Pictured are staff of Burns and McDonnell drafting blueprints for the buildings that were to be erected in the coming weeks. (Courtesy of the Museum of Missouri Military History.)

This photograph shows scores of vehicles lined up along a road at Camp Crowder as workers raised buildings. The work was not without incident, as a prefabricated roof for a mess hall collapsed during construction on October 25, 1941, resulting in the death of a 65-year-old worker from Topeka, Kansas, and sending three others to a Neosho hospital. (Courtesy of the Museum of Missouri Military History.)

One of the greatest challenges facing the crews during the early weeks of construction were the swampy conditions created by excessive rainfall; more than nine inches were received in the month of October 1941 alone. This photograph shows a bulldozer pulling a road grader to ensure crews could continue with the construction of the camp's roadways despite the wet conditions. (Courtesy of the Museum of Missouri Military History.)

Many factors went into the decision of where to locate the military post that would eventually become Camp Crowder. The camp was established approximately three miles southeast of Neosho because of its proximity to the St. Louis–San Francisco Railway and Kansas City Southern Railroad, which ran through the edge of the camp. There were 6.5 miles of spurs and sidings laid during the construction phase to deliver materials such as lumber used in constructing barracks and other facilities. (Courtesy of the Museum of Missouri Military History.)

Despite the wet conditions, dozens of trucks continued to pick up stacks of lumber delivered by the railroads to various locations in preparation for the construction of barracks and other camp buildings. It was reported that on November 11, 1941, there were 446 buildings under construction. (Courtesy of the Museum of Missouri Military History.)

In anticipation of the thousands of troops who would soon be passing through the camp, engineers designed an advanced sewage system consisting of 48 miles of concrete piping and nearly 600 manholes. Pictured here is the construction phase for one of the sewage disposal filtration systems, consisting of a submerged bed of rock that was used to process the waste generated throughout the camp. (Courtesy of the Museum of Missouri Military History.)

This photograph features one of the buildings that eventually became a service club on Camp Crowder. During World War II, Camp Crowder had four service clubs, each of which had its own guesthouse for the guests of soldiers stationed there. Service Clubs No. 1 and No. 2 had large cafeterias or ballrooms and libraries, while Service Clubs No. 3 and No. 4 had rooms for dancing and reading and cafeterias. All clubs had a principal hostess and assistants and remained open from 10:00 a.m. to 2:00 p.m. and 4:00 p.m. to 10:00 p.m. (Courtesy of the Museum of Missouri Military History.)

The *Macon Chronicle Herald* reported on December 15, 1941, that 685 buildings were under construction at Camp Crowder, 431 of which were under roof. The northern Missouri newspaper also noted that 19,744 workers were employed at the camp and another 1,769 had been requested through local unions and employment services. (Courtesy of the Museum of Missouri Military History.)

Total employment at Camp Crowder reached 14,644 according to the November 14, 1941, *Neosho Times*. While construction crews toiled on 10-hour shifts during the daylight hours to erect barracks such as those pictured here, other crews often worked during the night to perform a large part of the roadwork around the camp. (Courtesy of the Museum of Missouri Military History.)

The framework of barracks buildings began to take form on the camp in the late summer and fall of 1941, on sections of property that had previously been privately owned farmland. Many area farmers were not pleased with the prices offered for their land, which led to picketing against the Federal Government Land Acquisition Department in nearby Neosho. (Courtesy of the Museum of Missouri Military History.)

Construction crews scrambled to raise the walls for barracks on Camp Crowder during the fall of 1941 in anticipation of the arrival of troops in the coming weeks. By January 2, 1942, a total of 81 building were ready for occupancy, and by January 29, this number rose to an impressive 352 usable buildings. (Courtesy of the Museum of Missouri Military History.)

This photograph, taken on January 30, 1942, shows the construction of the four-lane main road (two lanes entering Camp Crowder and two lanes exiting) that was later named Lyon Drive. In the background is the North Underpass, which passed under the Kansas City Southern Railroad. In the right background are many of the buildings comprising the main section of the post. (Courtesy of the Museum of Missouri Military History.)

While the design and construction of the water system that would supply the camp was under way, buildings were being erected—a process that required water to mix the concrete for piers and foundations. Throughout the early months of construction, this water was supplied to the individual worksites by trucks with water tanks mounted on the back. (Courtesy of the Museum of Missouri Military History.)

The road leading to the magazine area on Camp Crowder is pictured on January 28, 1942. The magazine was a storage igloo built into the side of a hill where there was stowed various types of munitions and Chemical Agent Identification Sets (small glass containers filled with various chemical agents used in training). In July 1981, three National Guard soldiers were overcome by vapors from the ground while excavating near the magazine; their injuries were consistent with exposure to phosgene gas. (Courtesy of the Museum of Missouri Military History.)

The hospital area on Camp Crowder comprised 98 one-story buildings. To generate the substantial level of steam heat needed to support these facilities, a power plant was constructed in the hospital area in January 1942, with an exhaust stack 115 feet in height and nine feet in diameter. (Courtesy of the Museum of Missouri Military History.)

There were many challenges in providing a clean and reliable source of potable water for the camp, which in the end resulted in an elaborate design consisting of a diversion dam and three pumping stations. Pictured is the diversion dam built on Shoal Creek, which served as the source of water for Camp Crowder. (Courtesy of the Museum of Missouri Military History.)

The water that was pulled from Shoal Creek was pumped to a purification plant 2,000 feet away and from there traveled nearly six miles through an underground concrete reservoir to the camp. Once reaching the camp, it was pumped into two elevated tanks, one of which is pictured here. (Courtesy of the Museum of Missouri Military History.)

The true expanse of what Camp Crowder grew into during World War II can be seen in this photograph taken in January 1942. Rows upon rows of barracks, post exchanges, and medical facilities stretched as far as the eye could see, with the two water towers visible in the distance. (Courtesy of the Museum of Missouri Military History.)

Camp Crowder truly assumed the mantle of a spreading city that leaped into existence in a matter of months. When the primary phase of construction was completed in July 1942, there were 2,328 buildings in addition to 51 miles of new roads and 5 miles of new railroad tracks. (Courtesy Museum of Missouri Military History.)

One of the carpenter crews employed on the Camp Crowder project posed for this photograph on March 27, 1942, in front of some of the barracks they helped to construct. In December 1942, a stellar safety record was achieved despite high employment numbers. During this month, although employment spiked at around 20,000 with a total of nearly four million hours worked, there were only 72 injuries resulting in loss of time from the job—less than two injuries for every 100,000 hours of labor. (Author's collection.)

Two
Hustle and Bustle of Camp Life

Missouri governor Forrest C. Donnell was one of the guest speakers at the formal dedication ceremonies for Camp Crowder on April 12, 1942. During his dedicatory address, Donnell recognized not only the role the camp would serve in training soldiers for combat, but also acknowledged those who toiled in its construction. (Courtesy of Missouri State Archives.)

This postcard features the color guard that passed by the reviewing stand during the dedication ceremony for the newly constructed Camp Crowder on April 12, 1942. Following the address by Governor Donnell, the entire garrison at the camp passed in review for the governor and Gen. Walter E. Prosser, commanding officer. (Author's collection.)

Early in the development of Camp Crowder, a civilian police department was created to help keep the peace on the expanding military post and investigate any crimes or disturbances. In the months after the post was established, the civilian police force was replaced by military police; however, many of the former Camp Crowder police officers were later employed by local police departments in nearby communities such as Joplin and Carthage. (Courtesy of the Museum of Missouri Military History.)

The civilian police force on Camp Crowder was relatively short-lived; however, the military police that took its place remained actively involved in working with local police departments on several occasions. On December 31, 1942, Camp Crowder leadership anticipated some trouble, considering both the holiday and payday for the soldiers fell on the same date. As such, the camp placed 40 to 60 military policemen on duty on the post while providing military police to supplement the police forces of nearby Joplin and Neosho for the evening. (Courtesy the Museum of Missouri Military History.)

As Camp Crowder grew into a virtual city comprised of thousands of soldiers, Women's Army Corps (WACs), civilian employees, and POWs, fire protection became a major concern. In October 1942, the fire department on the camp was comprised of 57 trained civilian firefighters who operated from six fire stations around the post; a seventh station was added several weeks later. (Courtesy of the Museum of Missouri Military History.)

Col. George W. Teachout, who became commander of Camp Crowder on September 30, 1941, established a fire prevention program during the construction phase of the camp intended to prevent the "needless loss of life and property by fire and eliminating unsafe conditions," as reported by the *Neosho Daily News* on October 6, 1942. Pictured are members of the Camp Crowder Fire Department in 1942. (Courtesy Missouri State Archives.)

The group of buildings that comprised the hospital area included 45 wards, 4 administration buildings, 5 recreation buildings, 10 hospital barracks, 5 mess halls, and 10 officers' and nurses' quarters in addition to clinics, laboratories, and several buildings used for storage of medical supplies and equipment. Also included was a garage for six ambulances. (Author's collection.)

This postcard from the early 1940s shows one of the 14 chapels located on Camp Crowder during World War II; it could accommodate more than 400 persons. Each chapel featured a main congregational room, two chaplain's rooms, consultation room, vestibule, cloak room, and balcony. All of the chapels were constructed using the same set of blueprints and plans; however, the interior of each chapel could be personalized for each denomination or faith. (Author's collection.)

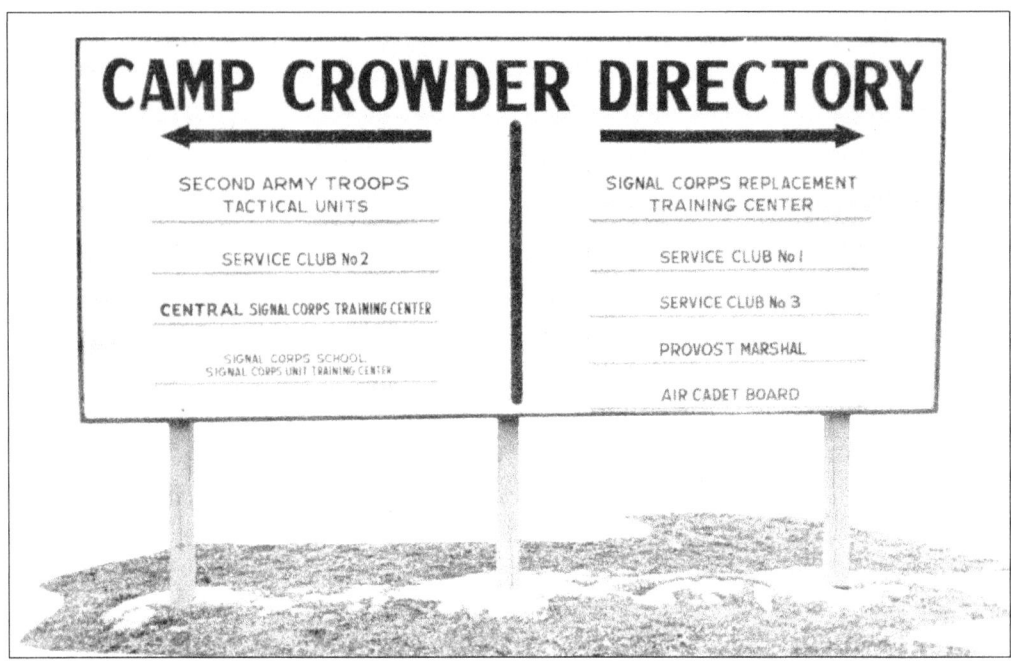

On a sprawling military post that at one time encompassed approximately 42,800 acres, it was often a challenge to find the way to one's intended destination. During World War II, Camp Crowder had several signs such as this to help direct soldiers and visitors to specific areas on the post. (Author's collection.)

Newly enlisted recruits are pictured upon their arrival at Camp Crowder for their basic course of instruction in August 1942. Approximately six months earlier, in February 1942, a group of recently arrived recruits became the first to begin their basic training at the camp. After successful completion of their initial military training, they were assigned to more advanced training in one of the Signal Corps' primary or support roles. (Courtesy Missouri State Archives.)

Fort Monmouth, New Jersey, opened as a replacement training center for the Signal Corps months before construction began on Camp Crowder. The training facilities in the Monmouth area eventually became the Eastern Signal Corps Center, while Signal Corps training facilities at Camp Crowder became the Midwestern Signal Corps Training Center, with a capacity for 6,000 students. (Courtesy Missouri State Archives.)

In order to administer the group of schools that would provide the training for the Signal Corps at Camp Crowder, in October 1942 the Midwestern Signal Corps Training Center was renamed Central Signal Corps Training Center. When the US Army realized that Fort Monmouth and Camp Crowder had exceeded their capacity for training soldiers to serve in the Signal Corps during the war, the Western Signal Corps Training Center was opened at Camp Kohler, California. (Courtesy Missouri State Archives.)

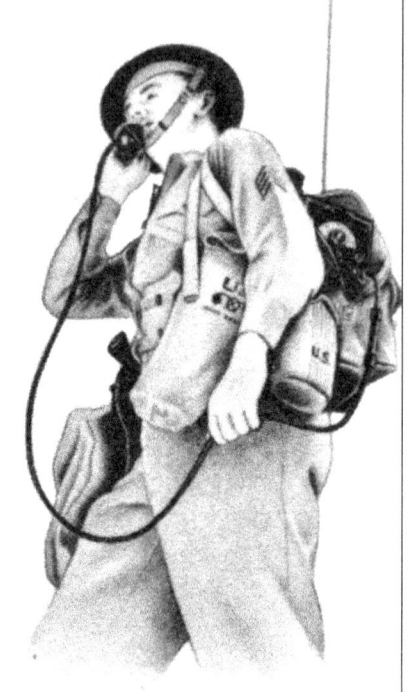

Initially, Camp Crowder was intended to serve as a joint training school for both the infantry and Signal Corps but eventually became a second replacement training center for the Signal Corps in early 1942. The Army Service Forces Training Center was established on the post and became the coordinating headquarters for the Basic and Specialist Unit Command, which coordinated for recruits their basic training (boot camp) followed by assignment to training in a Signal Corps specialty. (Author's collection.)

The motto and mission of the Signal Corps became "Get the Message Through." During World War II, the soldiers of the Signal Corps were responsible for establishing and maintaining the communication networks that connected the various components of the US Army, which included radio and telegraph operators, linemen, cable splicers, and installers. (Author's collection.)

A nine-week course of instruction was established at Camp Crowder for personnel and supply clerks, truck drivers, and typists. Students who were able to achieve a speed of 30 words per minute in the 30 hours in the typing course became eligible to attend the teletype course. Pictured here is Sergeant Valentine providing a block of instruction to students during a teletype class at the camp in 1944. (Courtesy Missouri State Archives.)

Typists were necessary for a range of administrative duties and filled such essential roles as personnel clerks, code clerks, and message center clerks, while teletypists were trained to process communications between field units and the War Department. (Author's collection.)

In this photograph taken on July 4, 1943, members of the Signal Corps are pictured routing telephone communications and performing maintenance on switchboards. Recruits with a distinct accent were often denied the opportunity to serve as switchboard operators during the war, regardless of any demonstrated ability in operating communication devices, to prevent the possibility of miscommunications. (Courtesy Missouri State Archives.)

The laying of telephone lines in a field environment, as featured in this Curt Teich postcard from the early 1940s, was one of the communication specialities taught at Signal Corps training centers. Camp Crowder initiated weekend field exercises in 1943 as a form of on-the-job training to provide soldiers with the experience of installing full-scale communication networks similar to those that might be used in a theater of war. (Author's collection.)

Signal Corps trainees received the opportunity to train with many developing technologies at the camp during World War II; one such piece of equipment was the facsimile machine. During the war, these machines were of demonstrated importance transmitting essential documents such as military orders in addition to weather charts and maps. (Courtesy Missouri State Archives.)

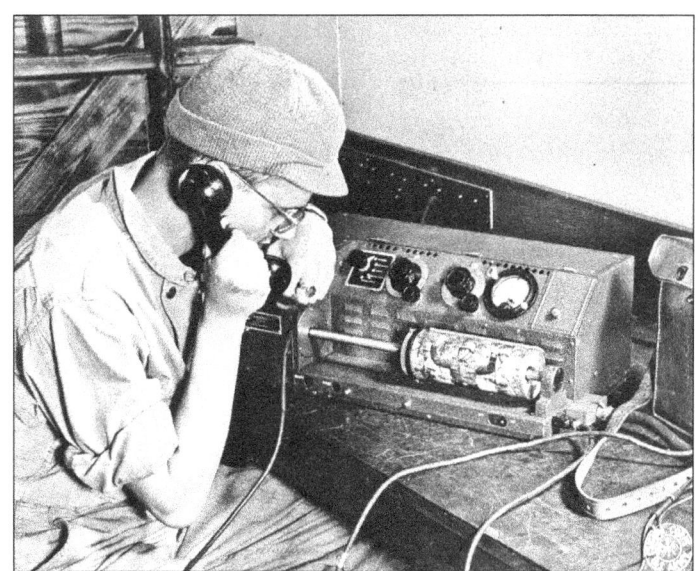

An integral aspect of field training was the message center, which was often set up under simulated combat conditions to prepare the soldiers for situations they might encounter overseas. The message center had the onerous task of receiving, encoding, decoding, relaying, and delivering messages to the proper headquarters, often in a matter of minutes, to ensure a smooth, uninterrupted flow of information. (Courtesy Missouri State Archives.)

This postcard from the early 1940s shows Signal Corps pole linemen stationed at Camp Crowder learning the process of climbing poles to install and repair communication lines. This training was conducted in a small section of the post where telephone poles were erected for the purpose. Many of the linemen who trained with the Wire Training Section at the camp later performed such installations and repairs in a combat environment. (Author's collection.)

Switchboards played a critical role in getting the message through for the Signal Corps, as operators were trained to place and answer calls, make the connections necessary to complete the circuit, and reroute communication traffic when circuits failed. Additionally, many trainees at Camp Crowder, such as those seen here, were trained to perform more detailed levels of maintenance on both static and field switchboard units. (Courtesy of Missouri State Archives.)

The Basic and Specialist Unit Command was comprised of 10 sections providing the following training: Clerks Training Section, Cooks Training Section, Motor Transport Section, Pigeon Breeding and Training Center Section, Radio Training Section, Signal Center Training Section, Typist and Teletype Training Section, Wire Training Section, and Band Training Section. Pictured are soldiers assigned to the Motor Transport Section at Camp Crowder undergoing instruction on the repair of US Army vehicles in 1942. (Courtesy of Missouri State Archives.)

The Motor Transport Section at Camp Crowder not only provided training to the mechanics who would keep the Army's vehicles running, but also provided a chauffeur's course to teach recruits how to operate the vehicles and perform basic, field-level repairs. Pictured is training being conducted at the camp during World War II to demonstrate how to assist vehicles across a ravine. (Courtesy of Missouri State Archives.)

Once training was completed in a chauffeur or automotive repair course, the soldiers were then assigned to a field unit to begin applying the skills they had recently acquired. Motor transport crews were placed in situations during which many problems they might encounter were simulated, providing them with the experience to operate and repair vehicles under a variety of conditions. (Courtesy of Missouri State Archives.)

This photograph was taken during a training exercise at Camp Crowder on June 30, 1944. Pictured are Signal Corps trainees aboard an assault boat learning to navigate through mine-laden waters to invade the hostile shores of Indian Creek. As part of their realistic training, they were instructed on how to establish a beachhead and set up a communications center. Due to the timing of the training cycle, these trainees missed one of the most profound amphibious operations of the war: the famed D-Day invasion took place six days later. (Courtesy of Museum of Missouri Military History.)

During the latter part of World War II, there were two regiments under the Medical Training Group—the 11th and 13th Medical Training Regiments. The primary function of the groups was to prepare medical aid personnel for service in redeployed units and units that might have to perform extended field service. Medical trainees are pictured in March 1945 demonstrating treatment for a wounded soldier during a field exercise at Camp Crowder. (Author's collection.)

The *Camp Crowder Message* became the post's official weekly newspaper and was distributed every Thursday. The first issue, pictured here, was printed on February 12, 1942, and as the post continued to grow during World War II, the paper garnered news items not only from its full-time staff but also through submissions provided by soldiers who served as reporters in every company on post. (Courtesy of Missouri State Archives.)

This photograph from the summer of 1944 shows WACs and soldiers stationed at Camp Crowder sorting mail for distribution. During the holidays, mail delivery could become a daunting task. As Christmas 1943 approached, the *Neosho Daily News* reported that 10 extra postal employees were added to the staff at the Neosho Post Office and 20 helpers were sent to the post office at Camp Crowder to assist with the influx of parcels and packages. (Courtesy Missouri State Archives.)

Col. Oveta Culp Hobby (first row, in uniform next to Colonel Teachout), pictured in August 1943 during a visit to Camp Crowder, was accompanied by more than two dozen women from throughout the United States who belonged to groups such as the American Farm Bureau Federation, the USO, and Daughters of the American Revolution. Colonel Hobby, who served as the commander-in-chief of the Women's Army Auxiliary Corps (WAACs), was visiting the camp to swear in more than 300 former WAACs into the Women's Army Corps (WACs), the latter of which became official on September 1, 1943. (Courtesy of Missouri State Archives.)

Maj. Gen. Clarence H. Danielson was commanding general of the Seventh Service Command, established in 1944 by the WAC Advisory Committee to further interest in the WACs. On June 2, 1944, thirteen women appointed by General Danielson to the committee completed a one-day tour of Camp Crowder to witness the work being performed by WACs on the post. Pictured in the first row, fifth from left, is Sarah Bowman of Iowa City, Iowa, who was state chairman of recruitment for the Iowa Federation of Women's Clubs. (Courtesy of the Missouri State Archives.)

Aside from the WAC training centers at Fort Des Moines, Iowa, and Fort Oglethorpe, Georgia, more WACs were stationed at Camp Crowder during the latter part of World War II than any other US Army post. Pictured is one of the dining facilities operated by WAC personnel who were stationed at Camp Crowder during the war. (Courtesy of the Missouri State Archives.)

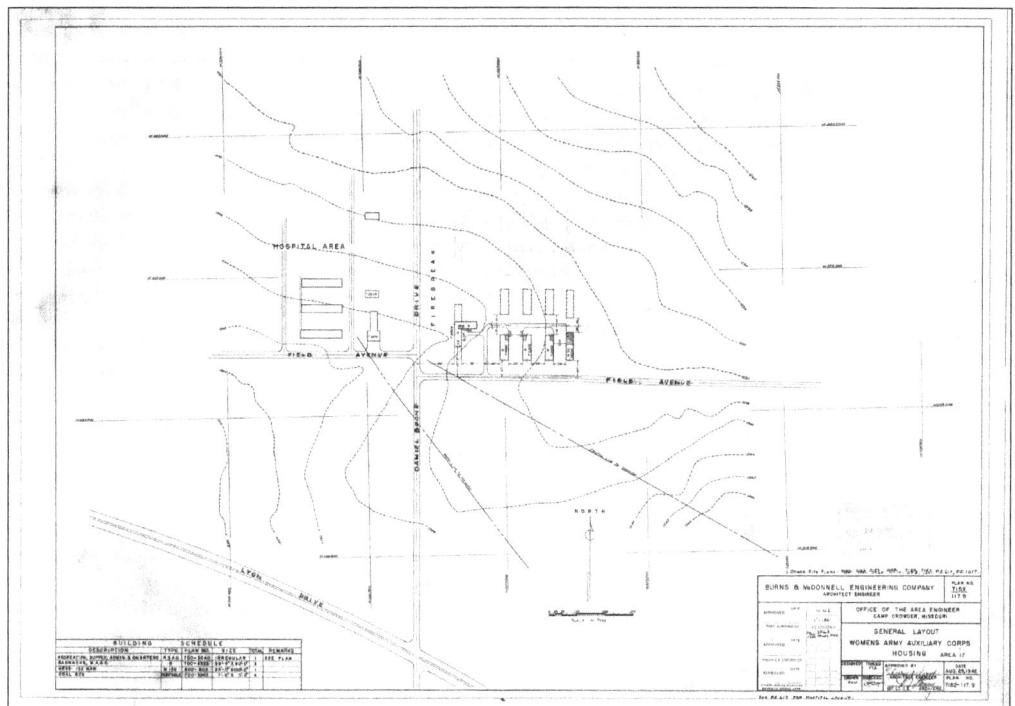

Original blueprints by Burns and McDonnell Engineering Company, dated August 29, 1942, show the planned layout of the WAAC housing area, east of the hospital complex at the junction of Daniel Boone Drive and Field Avenue on Camp Crowder. The first contingent of WAACs would begin arriving approximately five months later, in February 1943. (Courtesy of Museum of Missouri Military History.)

Sgt. Johna Pimper, a post photographer for Camp Crowder, snapped this humorous photograph in October 1943 to help demonstrate that the camp was home to possibly the tallest and shortest chaplains in the US Army. Garner D. Noland, left, a chaplain for the camp hospital, stood 5 feet, 2 1/2 inches tall. His counterpart, Frederick G. Nichols, served as chaplain at Chapel 3677 on post and was an impressive 6 feet, 4 1/2 inches tall. (Courtesy of Missouri State Archives.)

Addison "Mort" Walker was attending the University of Missouri when he was drafted into the US Army in 1943. The Kansas City native completed his boot camp in Florida and from there was transferred to Camp Crowder for signal training. While he was at the camp, there was flooding around the barracks that provided Walker with the idea for "Camp Swampy"—the fictional military camp featured in his *Beetle Bailey* comic strip. (Courtesy of Mort Walker.)

"HE GOT A LETTER FROM HIS GIRL"

Prior to his induction into the US Army, Mort Walker had achieved a certain level of success with his cartooning. While he was stationed at Camp Crowder for several weeks in 1943, he continued to refine his cartooning skills, as featured in this humorous drawing of camp life. Walker would later complete Army training at Washington University in St. Louis, where he met a sergeant who inspired the Sgt. Snorkel character in *Beetle Bailey*. (Courtesy of Mort Walker.)

Mort Walker is pictured at his home in Stamford, Connecticut, in October 2017 holding a vintage "Sweetheart Pillow" that was sold in the post exchanges at Camp Crowder during World War II. After the war, Walker returned to the University of Missouri to finish his education before moving to Connecticut, where he carried forth the Camp Crowder legacy through *Beetle Bailey*. Sadly, Walker passed away in January 2018. (Author's collection.)

Pvt. Edward Egg of Erie, Pennsylvania, is pictured at Camp Crowder in June 1944 with his invention, which, he explained, helped him travel 9,000 miles before the war. The creative device consists of a box with a glass tube inside in the shape of a hitchhiker's hand and thumb, powered by batteries and a spark coil. There is a button beside the handle that he could push to illuminate the hand whenever a vehicle approached. Full of character, Private Egg demonstrated the most effective pose to use when a ride was needed. (Courtesy of Museum of Missouri Military History.)

A bus carrying 26 soldiers and a WAC private from a New Year's Eve celebration at Joplin crashed head-on into a concrete bridge abutment on Highway 71, a quarter-mile north of the main entrance at Camp Crowder, at 5:05 a.m. on January 1, 1944. A soldier from Massachusetts was killed in the accident, while another had to be extricated from the wreckage with an acetylene torch. (Courtesy of Missouri State Archives.)

After striking the abutment, the back end of the bus slid into the ditch, causing the occupants to be thrown violently into a heap among the wreckage; however, the bus somehow remained upright. A second soldier, Pvt. Richard Fischel, perished at the Camp Crowder hospital on January 2, 1944, and, sadly, the death toll grew to three when Pfc. Frank J. Cenyuka died at the camp hospital on January 3. (Courtesy of Missouri State Archives.)

In this photograph from May 1943, soldiers from Camp Crowder are assembled in preparation for the anticipated flooding in the region. The waters of Shoal Creek rose to the extent that power lines were washed away, requiring electric service to be redirected to Neosho and Camp Crowder from alternate power stations in locations such as Diamond, Missouri. City residents were asked to curtail their water usage during this period because the power shortage inhibited water pumping in the area. (Courtesy of Missouri State Archives.)

Soldiers from Camp Crowder dug drainage ditches along the railroad tracks on and near Camp Crowder to help curtail the rising floodwaters in May 1943. The efforts to stop the damage from the swollen rivers did not fully succeed, as Frisco Railway service in both directions out of Neosho was interrupted for several days due to the record flooding. It was the flooding during this period that inspired Mort Walker's "Camp Swampy" in *Beetle Bailey*. (Courtesy of Missouri State Archives.)

An often forgotten fact is that China was an ally of the United States during World War II, from shortly after the Japanese attack on Pearl Harbor until the surrender of Japan in 1945. Many Chinese soldiers were sent to train at various US bases, including Camp Crowder, where the soldiers pictured learned to perform maintenance and repairs on various types of military vehicles. (Courtesy of Missouri State Archives.)

Many civilians in Joplin and the surrounding communities contributed to the war effort. Pictured is Walter J. Nickel, who served as the superintendent of cold storage equipment at the camp. Nickel received a $200 prize for "improvement on methods for re-operation of refrigeration coil assemblies," according to the December 30, 1944, *Neosho Daily News*. He became active in the War Dads Chapter of Joplin after his son Wallace E. Nickel left their Joplin home to attend the US Military Academy in the summer of 1944. (Courtesy of Missouri State Archives.)

The obstacle course became a principal element of the training provided to soldiers at the camp in World War II. Three quarters of a mile in length, the course consisted of walls, hurdles, streams, and barriers. Pictured here are soldiers in the Reconditioning Section of Camp Crowder navigating the obstacle course as they push themselves to their physical limits. Those assigned to the Reconditioning Section were recovering from wounds and injuries sustained during their military service. (Courtesy Missouri State Archives.)

Soldiers assigned to the Reconditioning Section are pictured in July 1943 jumping the ropes on one of the post's obstacle courses. The following year, the Reconditioning Section at Camp Crowder held an open house to exhibit mass calisthenics, obstacle courses, and gymnastic drills used to help convalescing soldiers return to active duty. (Courtesy of Missouri State Archives.)

During an event recognized as Infantry Day, Col. George W. Teachout, commandant of Camp Crowder, welcomed citizens of Neosho and the surrounding areas to the camp on June 15, 1944, to witness several military demonstrations, ceremonies, and exhibits. Pictured here are local residents watching as soldiers crawl 80 yards under a barrage of machine gun fire as part of the post's battle conditioning course. (Courtesy Missouri State Archives.)

It was estimated that more than 8,000 people attended the Infantry Day events at Camp Crowder on June 15, 1944. Although a number of demonstrations were held to show the rigorous training received by the soldiers, which included a pass and review of 10,000 troops, it was reported that the sentry dogs that were trained on the post as part of the Army's K-9 Corps were the most popular attraction of the day. (Courtesy of the Missouri State Archives.)

Soldiers assigned to Camp Crowder provide a weapons demonstration to members of the public attending an open house on March 9, 1945. In addition to a number of demonstrations and a retreat parade performed by soldiers of the 800th Signal Training Regiment, Maj. Gen. Walter E. Prosser, commanding general of the camp, provided a brief address. (Courtesy of the Missouri State Archives.)

Three
LEADERSHIP

Congressman Dewey Short represented Missouri's Seventh District when he sponsored legislative action in 1941 for the placement of a Signal Corps training center in his beloved Ozarks. The US representative was often described as a "silvery-tongued orator" and carried much influence as the longtime minority-ranking member of the House Armed Services Committee. One of the most popular politicians from the Ozarks, the Galena, Missouri, native served a total of 24 years in Congress. He is pictured shaking hands with Major General Prosser while visiting Camp Crowder in August 1943. (Courtesy of Missouri State Archives.)

Brig. Gen. Frank C. Meade was transferred from Washington, DC, where he served in the office of the chief signal officer, to become commanding general of the Midwestern Signal Corps Replacement Training Center at Camp Crowder on December 29, 1942. A 1917 graduate of the US Military Academy at West Point, General Meade first served in the coastal artillery and in 1926 began his association with the signal corps. (Courtesy of Missouri State Archives.)

On January 2, 1942, Brig. Gen. William Samuel Rumbough became commanding general of the Midwestern Signal Corps Replacement Training Center at Camp Crowder. Rumbough's assumption of command came on the heels of an order that shifted the emphasis of training at the camp from infantry to the signal corps. A few months after arriving at Camp Crowder, Rumbough became the chief signal officer in the European theater of operations and was promoted to major general. (Courtesy of Missouri State Archives.)

Maj. Gen. Walter E. Prosser became the new commanding general of Camp Crowder as well as commandant of the Signal Corps Replacement Training Center on March 30, 1942. Prosser replaced Brig. Gen. William Rumbough, who reverted to the position of commanding general of the Signal Corps Replacement Training Center. (Courtesy Missouri State Archives.)

Maj. Gen. Walter E. Prosser, right, is pictured in September 1944 granting his well wishes to members of a soldier chorus as they depart for Omaha, Nebraska. In October 1942, Prosser became commanding general of the Midwestern Signal Corps Training Center, which then had three units placed under it—the Midwestern Signal Corps Replacement Training Center, the Midwestern Signal Corps School, and the Midwestern Signal Corps Unit Training Center. (Courtesy of Missouri State Archives.)

Pauline Davis Rumbough, the wife of Brig. Gen. William Samuel Rumbough, left, is pictured cutting the ribbon during the dedicatory rites at one of the seven post chapels on February 26, 1942. To the right are Lt. Col. John Williamson, post chaplain, and Lt. Col. C.O. Purdy (far right), chaplain for the Seventh Corps Area. Less than two weeks later, the first camp theater opened for business. (Courtesy Missouri State Archives.)

Brig. Gen. Charles M. Milliken came to Camp Crowder from the Office of the Chief Signal Officer in Washington, DC, in January 1943 and assumed the role of commanding general of the newly renamed Central Signal Corps Replacement Training Center. A 1914 graduate of West Point, Milliken served in both the infantry and Signal Corps branches during World War I. (Courtesy Missouri State Archives.)

Brig. Gen. Terence John Tully transferred to Camp Crowder in June 1945 to assume command of the Army Service Forces Training Center (ASFTC). At the time, the ASFTC at Camp Crowder was the largest Signal Corps and medical training installation. Tully's tenure at the Neosho camp was brief, however, as he was transferred to Army Service Forces headquarters in Washington, DC, in November 1945. (Courtesy Missouri State Archives.)

Maj. Gen. Dawson Olmstead, chief of the Signal Corps in Washington, DC, visited Camp Crowder in June 1942. During his visit, Olmstead reviewed the entire garrison during ceremonies that were open to the public. Olmstead went on to lead the Signal Corps through the largest part of World War II until retiring in January 1944. (Courtesy Missouri State Archives.)

Col. Alfred E. Larabee, far right, shakes hands with Maj. Gen. Walter E. Prosser at Camp Crowder in 1945. Larabee was transferred to Camp Crowder in January 1943 from the Signal Corps unit of the ROTC program at the University of California at Berkeley to serve as chief of staff of the Central Signal Corps Replacement Training Center. A veteran of World War I, Larabee went on to serve as chief executive officer of Camp Crowder before retiring in November 1945. (Courtesy of Missouri State Archives.)

Col. Sol P. Fink, pictured at Camp Crowder in 1944, enlisted in the United States Cavalry at the age of 14 and served in the Mexican Border Campaign, World War I, World War II, and Korea. During World War II, he served as a colonel in the Signal Corps and was stationed at Camp Crowder, where he became commander of signal training regiments. Following the war, he was a stockbroker in New York and passed away in Massachusetts in 1975 at 77 years of age. (Courtesy of Missouri State Archives.)

The 800th Signal Training Regiment was stationed at Camp Crowder during the latter part of World War II and "provided technical training in radio operations, radio repair, high power station operation and maintenance," according to the Army Historical Foundation. Members of the regiment are pictured in May 1945 receiving an address by their commander, Col. Sol P. Fink. (Courtesy of Missouri State Archives.)

Lt. Col. Francis A. Rickly was one of the first officers to arrive at Camp Crowder on December 6, 1941, the day prior to the attack on Pearl Harbor. He was appointed the assistant post executive officer and became executive officer on April 11, 1942. He was appointed the executive officer for station complement units following a reorganization of the post's administrative structure on July 6, 1944. On April 20, 1945, he was appointed to the position of individual services officer, but his lengthy association with Camp Crowder ended in mid-May 1945 when he left the post for another duty station. (Courtesy of the Missouri State Archives.)

Pictured in December 1944 shortly after his transfer to Camp Crowder, Col. James B. Haskell previously served as executive officer and commander of Fort Monmouth, New Jersey. Colonel Haskell, following his arrival at Camp Crowder, assumed duties as post executive officer, which he continued until retiring from the US Army on August 31, 1946. He passed away in 1985 and is buried in the cemetery of the US Military Academy in West Point. (Courtesy of Missouri State Archives.)

On April 1, 1946, Col. John B. Murphy became commandant of Camp Crowder, succeeding Brig. Gen. Charles E. Milliken, who received orders for Camp Polk, Louisiana. Prior to his arrival in Neosho, Murphy served overseas in World War II as an artillery commander for the 100th Infantry Division and later joined up with the Seventh Army in its drive to Stuttgart, Germany. (Courtesy of Missouri State Archives.)

From 1934 to 1940, Robert A. Rollison was an instructor of military science at the former Christian Brothers' College in St. Louis. Prior to World War II, he was a sergeant in the US Army but in 1940 was commissioned as a major in the Reserve Corps. Rollison served time as the post adjutant at Fort Leonard Wood before transferring to Camp Crowder in October 1941, where he became camp adjutant under Col. George W. Teachout. (Courtesy Missouri State Archives.)

A veteran of World Wars I and II, Lt. Col. Edward I. Pratt is pictured in July 1944 as he prepared to retire from the US Army as the public relations officer at Camp Crowder. Following his retirement, Pratt returned to his previous position with the public relations department of the Western Electric Company in New York. The veteran passed away in 1952 and was laid to rest in Forest Home Cemetery in Milwaukee, Wisconsin. (Courtesy of Missouri State Archives.)

Brig. Gen. Harry C. Ingles, right, is pictured with Maj. Gen. Walter E. Prosser on August 24, 1944. Ingles was serving as the chief signal officer for the US Army and was visiting Camp Crowder for a brief inspection tour of signal corps installations and training activities, which included the inspection of classrooms and field training exercises. (Courtesy of Missouri State Archives.)

Lt. Col. Thomas D. Mitchell is pictured in March 1946 shortly before leaving Camp Crowder for an assignment in the Chinese theater of operations. Mitchell served as an enlisted soldier in the Texas National Guard during the Mexican Border Campaign and as a second lieutenant with the 36th Division in France during World War I. He came to Camp Crowder on February 14, 1944, after the closing of the Army Radio School in Kansas City, and spent the next 25 months as post adjutant. (Courtesy of Missouri State Archives.)

Four
ENTERTAINMENT, CELEBRITIES, AND RECREATION

A native of Huron, South Dakota, where he was employed as manager of the local J.C. Penney store, Maj. Roy J. Miller became an exchange recreational officer with the exchange administration headquarters at Camp Crowder in the spring of 1943. One of the programs he helped oversee was the collection of donations on the post to purchase approximately 50,000 cigarettes in October 1944, which were sent to Americans serving overseas. In the same month, he appointed Bill Gukeisen, who had operated skating rinks in St. Louis, to manage the Spot—a 50- by 132-foot hardwood skating ring on Camp Crowder. (Author's collection.)

During the construction boom that took place at Camp Crowder in late 1941 and into early 1942, this impressive sports arena was erected with an arched roof and a 100- by 180-foot maple floor. The arena was large enough that three basketball games could be played simultaneously. When events were held in the center of the floor, knock-down bleachers could be set up to accommodate up to 4,000 spectators. (Author's collection.)

During World War II, soldiers training at Camp Crowder availed themselves of the bus service that ran between the post and locations in the nearby community of Neosho. During the war, the camp had theaters and other recreational activities available; however, the soldiers enjoyed their time away from Crowder by visiting the USO Club in Neosho as well as sites in nearby Joplin. (Courtesy of Missouri State Archives.)

Frank Rankmaster is pictured operating the switchboard during a USO show in Theater No. 2 in September 1944. Actor, director, and writer Carl Reiner served at the camp during World War II and was assigned to a Special Services unit—an entertainment branch of the US Army. His experiences at Camp Crowder would later be used in story lines for the character Rob Petrie played by Dick Van Dyke in *The Dick Van Dyke Show*. (Courtesy of Missouri State Archives.)

An exciting aspect of being stationed at Camp Crowder during World War II were the visits made by celebrities. Pictured is Colonel Teachout, far right, post commander of Camp Crowder, along with his wife and Eddie Bracken. A child actor in the 1920s, Bracken gained notoriety in the early 1940s starring in several light comedies. Bracken passed away in 2002 at 87, having enjoyed an acting career of more than 70 years. (Courtesy of Missouri State Archives.)

Kathryn Grayson, an American actress who appeared in several popular musicals and films, visited Camp Crowder in July 1943. During her visit, she performed a number of shows for the troops at recreational halls, service clubs, and the camp hospital. She is pictured sitting next to her husband, Lt. John S. Price, a movie star better known as John S. Shelton, who was stationed at Camp Crowder during the war. (Courtesy of Missouri State Archives.)

Allen Hermes was a painter and sculptor stationed at Camp Crowder with Headquarters Company, 800th Signal Training Regiment. He is pictured in May 1943 with a mural he painted of the midnight ride of Paul Revere while stationed at the camp, which was displayed in the recreation hall of the 800th Signal Training Regiment. In the years after the war, Hermes and his wife settled in Redding, Connecticut, where he continued to paint and teach until his passing in 2004. (Courtesy of Missouri State Archives.)

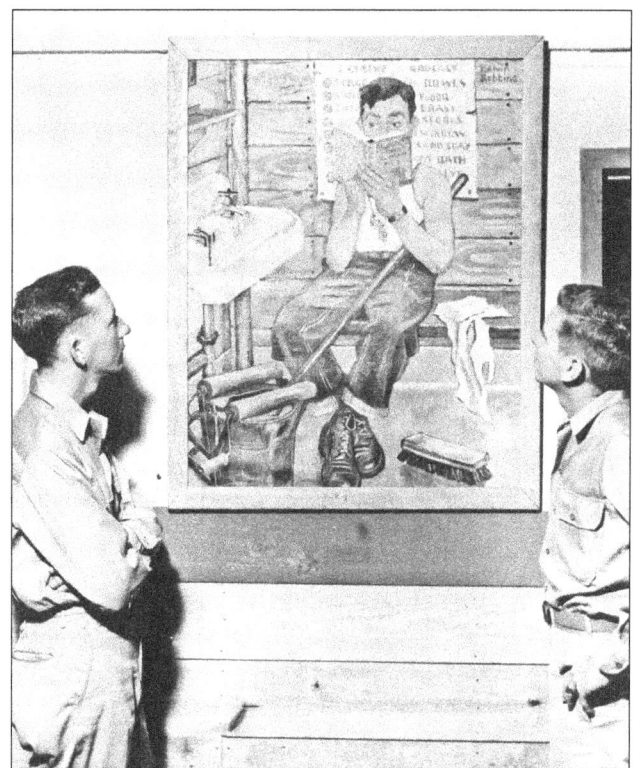

Life magazine held an art competition for service members stationed at Camp Crowder and *Latrine Orderly*, pictured here, was one of five prize-winning paintings. Often, the murals were hung for display in company dayrooms or other prominent locations on post. Pictured are Pvt. Edward Van Hooser (left) and Pvt. Everett Templeton of Company A, 31st Signal Training Battalion, viewing *Latrine Orderly*, which was on display in the post library of Service Club No. 1 on July 22, 1943. (Courtesy of Missouri State Archives.)

In 1943, a 60-piece band was organized at Camp Crowder from the Band Training Section at the Central Signal Corps Replacement Training Center. The band played concerts to entertain soldiers on the post and participated in a number of local events, including playing a concert at an open house for the Neosho USO on March 28, 1943. In the foreground is Capt. Joseph E. Skornicka (left), the band's chief, and Lt. Henry A. Klie (right), his assistant. (Courtesy of Missouri State Archives.)

Benny Goodman was a clarinetist and bandleader who earned the title "King of Swing" after rising to popularity with a number of hit songs in the 1930s. The celebrity and his band were scheduled to perform for the troops on the parade ground at Camp Crowder on September 24, 1942, but the show was moved indoors to the field house because of cold weather. (Courtesy of Missouri State Archives.)

Hollywood icon Cary Grant paid a four-day visit to Camp Crowder in March 1943. Grant, who was born in England and became an American citizen in 1942, participated in a number of tours of military bases to provide entertainment to the troops supporting the war effort. While at Camp Crowder, Grant not only put on shows, he also ate meals with the troops and visited a battalion on bivouac. (Courtesy of Missouri State Archives.)

One of the celebrity visits to Camp Crowder occurred on December 8, 1943, a little more than two years following the arrival of the first troops. On this date, heavyweight boxing champion Joe Louis visited the camp as part of a nationwide tour of military bases. During his visit, a record crowd of more than 5,000 spectators jammed the field house as Louis, left, sparred with Pfc. Booker T. Laster of the 804th Signal Training Regiment. (Courtesy of Missouri State Archives.)

There were many recreational activities that the soldiers of Camp Crowder enjoyed by traveling to the surrounding communities; however, there were also many activities provided on the post to keep the soldiers entertained when not engaged in training. The eight-lane bowling center, pictured on May 1, 1944, provided the trainees with many hours of enjoyment. (Courtesy of Missouri State Archives.)

The post exchanges on Camp Crowder were not only a place for soldiers to purchase ice cream, soda, magazines, and gifts for family or loved ones, they also became venues for small entertainment events. Pictured here is a musical show that was held at Post Exchange No. 2 on March 9, 1944, performed by a number of soldiers assigned to the camp. (Courtesy of Missouri State Archives.)

During its heyday in World War II, the hospital at Camp Crowder consisted of a medical screening center, three dental clinics, and several unit infirmaries located throughout the camp. Patients recovering from wounds and injuries and preparing to return to civilian life or military duty became part of the Reconditioning Section, a program of focused exercises, games, calisthenics, and recreational activities. Soldiers in the Reconditioning Service are pictured on a fishing trip at the camp in May 1945. (Courtesy of Missouri State Archives.)

Five

PRISONERS OF WAR

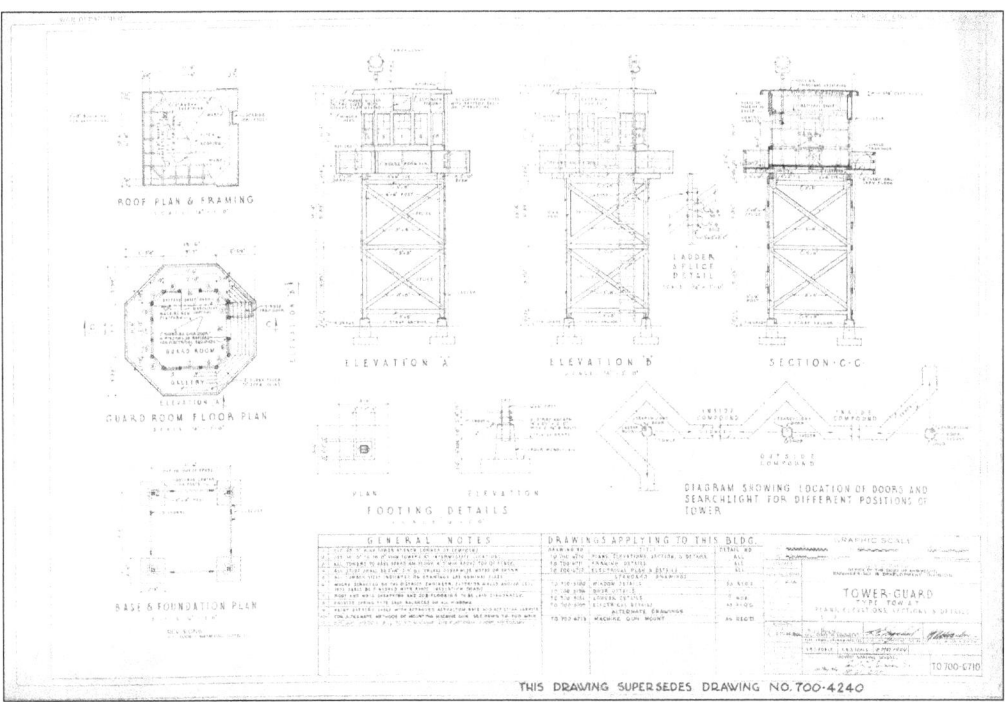

An additional mission was given to Camp Crowder when the first group of 443 German and Austrian POWs arrived on October 6, 1943, a few days after the completion of the stockade. The captured Austrian troops were moved to a different camp the following month. Pictured is the blueprint approved by the War Department's Office of Chief Engineers outlining the "plans, elevations, sections and details" in the construction of the guard towers for POW stockades. (Courtesy of Museum of Missouri Military History.)

The Geneva Convention called for physical and mental stimulus of POWs, and the Germans held at Camp Crowder were kept busy through assignment to several different projects on the post, including the construction of waterways lined and tiled with native stone. There are areas on both Camp Crowder and Crowder College where the remnants of these projects can still be seen. (Courtesy of Missouri State Archives.)

When deciding where to place POW camps, the government chose Camp Crowder because it was an existing military facility with available space in an isolated location. There was a high rate of participation in labor programs that provided POWs the opportunity to work outside the compound in a number of trades, such as working on automobiles in the post engineer paint shop. (Courtesy of Missouri State Archives.)

An article in the *Camp Crowder Message*—the official weekly newspaper of the post—noted that officials estimated the employment of POWs in various tasks around the post saved an estimated $38,000 each week. POWs are pictured on November 22, 1944, preparing loaves of bread in the post bakery. (Courtesy of Missouri State Archives.)

The simplest means by which to identify POWs on Camp Crowder and several other military posts were the letters "PW" on their outfits. POWs are pictured wearing these letters on their work outfits while on an "ash and trash" detail (picking up litter or cigarette butts) around the barracks in November 1944. (Courtesy of Missouri State Archives.)

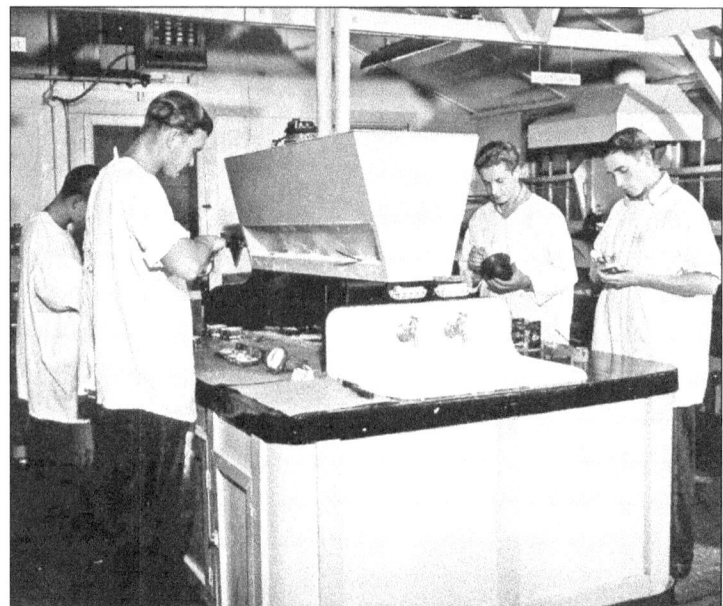

Shortly after POWs arrived at Camp Crowder, a survey was conducted to assess their educational background and civilian and military employment experiences to determine the best fit for them within the camp's labor program. Those with a medical background were placed at the post hospital or other related areas, such as these POWs who received assignment as dental technicians in the dental lab. (Courtesy of Missouri State Archives.)

POWs were not required to work; however, those who chose to were employed for eight-hour workdays and received a payment of 80¢ a day, such as the POWs pictured here, who were assigned to the post engineer carpenter shop. Those who chose not to work or who were in treatment for a medical condition or injuries received 10¢ a day. The payment was made in coupons that could be redeemed at a canteen for items like candy, tobacco, and soft drinks. (Courtesy of Missouri State Archives.)

The post utilities paint shop employed a number of prisoners of war who plied their skills in painting doors and other materials used in construction of buildings on the post. The size of the internment camp at Camp Crowder doubled in the spring of 1945 to accommodate an additional 1,000 POWS. More than 2,000 prisoners were held by the time the final 212 Germans left Camp Crowder on May 7, 1946. (Courtesy of Missouri State Archives.)

A funeral was held in April 1944 for a German prisoner of war who passed away at Camp Crowder. Ludwig Krause, a prisoner who was acting as the spokesperson for the German POW camp, led an open-air ceremony to honor their departed comrade. The remains of the deceased were then transported to Camp Clark for internment in their POW cemetery since Camp Crowder did not maintain burial grounds. (Courtesy of Missouri State Archives.)

Although German POWs fulfilled a number of employment roles at Camp Crowder, including working in the many warehouses on the post, a change in War Department policy created a temporary labor crisis. As noted in the *Joplin Globe* on July 28, 1945, "300 to 500 more civilian workers are immediately needed at Camp Crowder to take the place of prisoners of war who will be removed from all jobs that can be filled by discharged veterans or civilian employees." (Courtesy of Missouri State Archives.)

This map shows the former location of the two prisoner of war camps on Camp Crowder as they appeared in 1945. When the war ended and the POW operations were shut down in May 1946, the buildings that once housed the prisoners were dismantled and sent to the University of Missouri and other institutions of higher learning to be used as housing for veterans pursuing an education. A portion of the property that once housed POW Camp No. 1 on Radio Road is now utilized by the Neosho Public Works Department. (Author's collection.)

Remnants of the building once utilized by German POWs as a schoolhouse on Camp Crowder still stand on an overgrown section of property owned by the Missouri National Guard. During World War II, several of the instructors were German internees who served as educators prior to the war. They helped direct classes for POWs at the camp in various subjects like English, history, math, shorthand, and several technical fields. (Author's collection.)

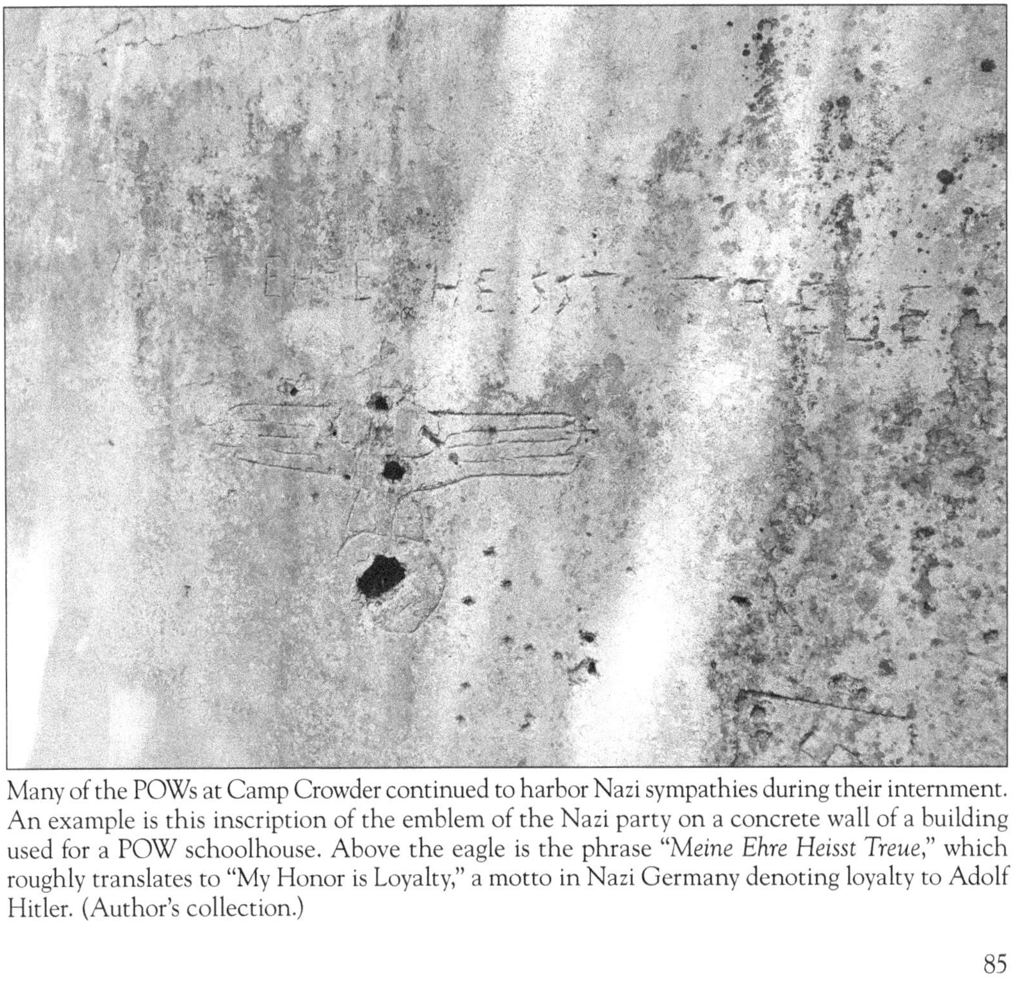

Many of the POWs at Camp Crowder continued to harbor Nazi sympathies during their internment. An example is this inscription of the emblem of the Nazi party on a concrete wall of a building used for a POW schoolhouse. Above the eagle is the phrase "*Meine Ehre Heisst Treue*," which roughly translates to "My Honor is Loyalty," a motto in Nazi Germany denoting loyalty to Adolf Hitler. (Author's collection.)

On April 10, 1944, German POW Helmut Rumesch sent this letter from Camp Crowder to his parents in Raimundgasse, Germany (now Austria), thanking them for the letters they had sent and advising them of his condition. Letters sent from POWs were reviewed by both German and US censors to ensure no compromising information was being transmitted either overtly or covertly. (Author's collection.)

Six

Memorabilia

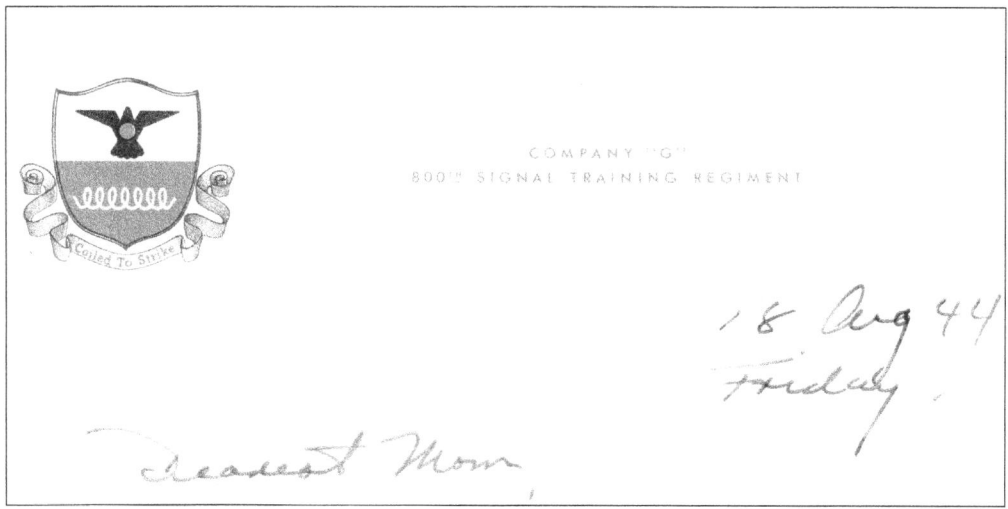

During the training cycle at Camp Crowder, draftees and enlistees rarely found the opportunity to use a phone unless they were given a pass to visit a nearby town such as Carthage or Neosho. As such, the primary means of communication became letters written by hand. A number of different types of letterhead emerged from Camp Crowder during World War II, including those specific to individual units, such as this letterhead from Company G, 800th Signal Training Regiment. (Author's collection.)

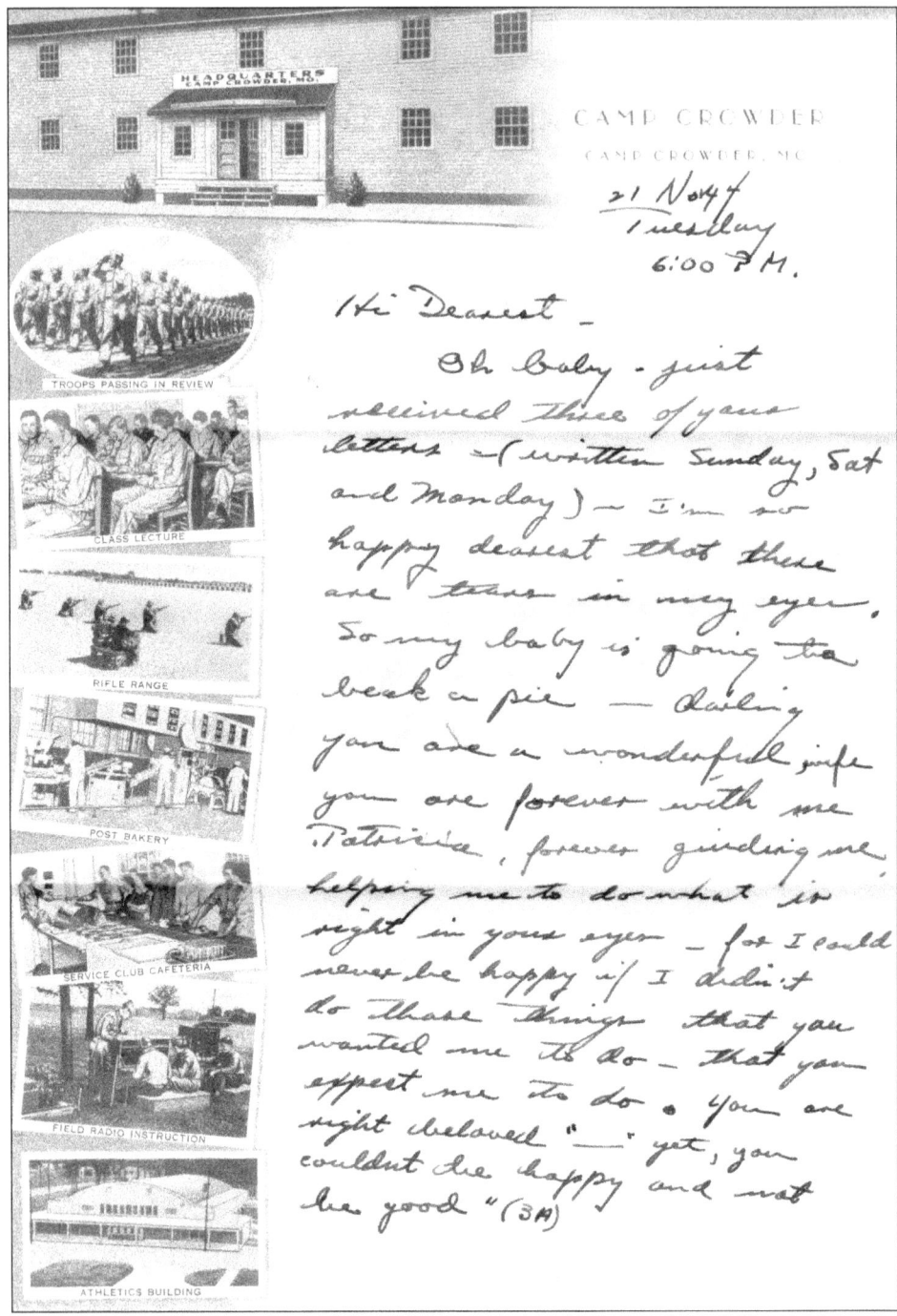

Henry H. Gatter was stationed at Camp Crowder in November 1944 with Company C, 3102nd Signal Service Battalion when he mailed this letter to his wife in Pennsylvania on letterhead available for purchase at many of the exchanges on the post. Weeks prior to this, many of his letters responded to his wife's interest in moving to Neosho to be with her husband; however, Gatter explained, the local "housing situation is terrible . . . the camp is now many times its original population." (Author's collection.)

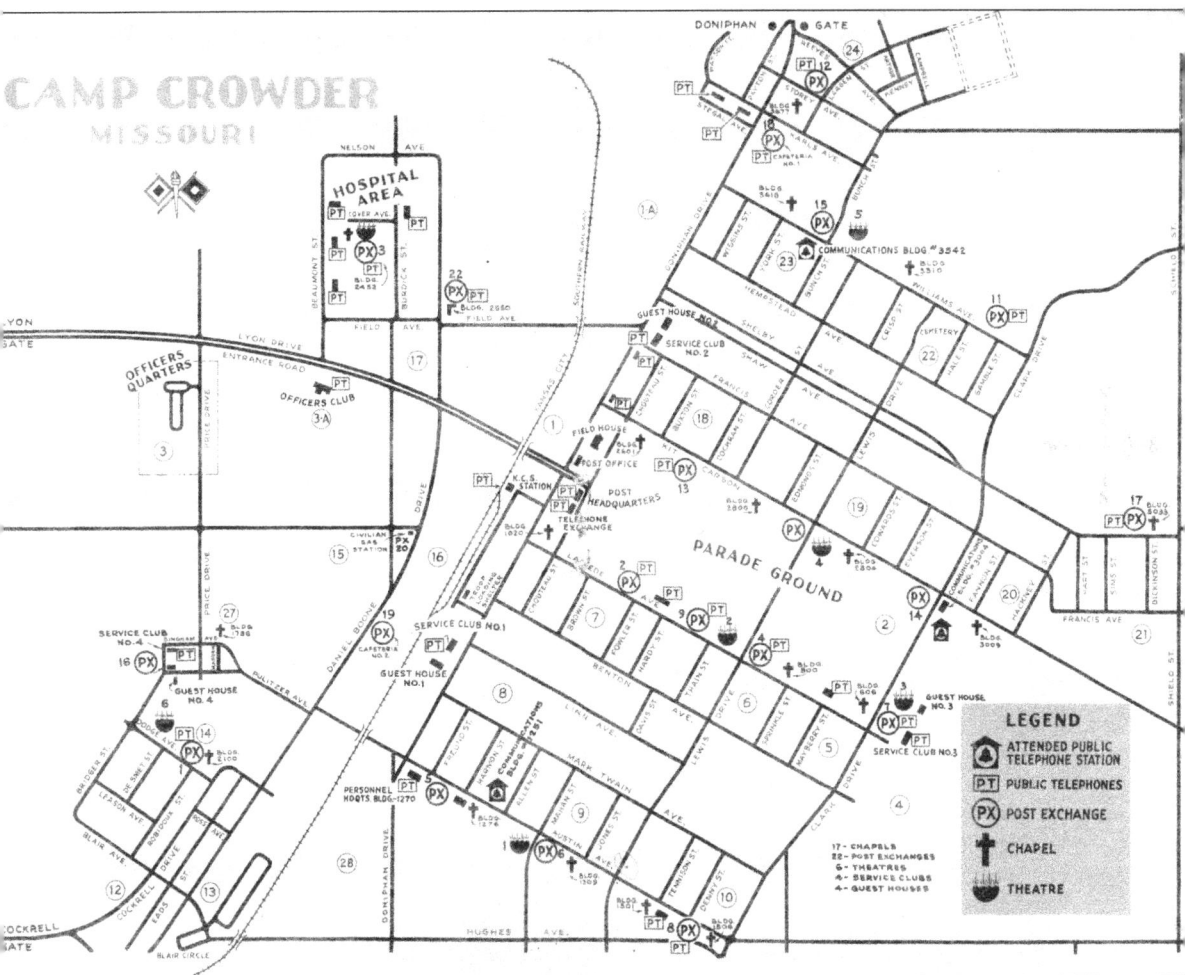

The Southwestern Bell Telephone Company printed maps such as these that were included in a small informational booklet provided to new arrivals at Camp Crowder during World War II. This 1943 map shows the layout of the primary streets on the camp in addition to the location of notable buildings and facilities such as the camp headquarters, post exchanges, theaters, and service clubs. (Author's collection.)

The Medical Training Group was activated at Camp Crowder in early 1945 under the command of Col. Frank Matlack. The group was initially comprised of a detachment of the medical training units stationed at Camp Barkley, Texas, that arrived at Camp Crowder in March 1945 and soon began providing training to recruits who would become medics for the US Army. Pictured is one of the training manuals issued at the camp. (Author's collection.)

Charley Caduce was a cartoon character developed by the Army Service Forces Training Center at Camp Crowder to demonstrate in training booklets a number of medical proficiencies to be learned by medics. While stationed at the camp, medical trainees learned emergency care and treatment of casualties, including how to treat various types of wounds and administer morphine for pain. (Author's collection.)

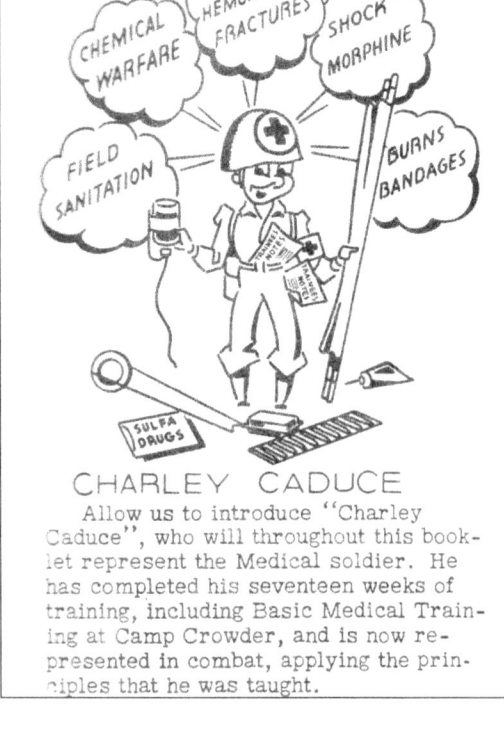

CHARLEY CADUCE

Allow us to introduce "Charley Caduce", who will throughout this booklet represent the Medical soldier. He has completed his seventeen weeks of training, including Basic Medical Training at Camp Crowder, and is now represented in combat, applying the principles that he was taught.

This is the cover of a songbook printed at Camp Crowder and distributed to each member of the contingent of WACs stationed at post. It is estimated that more than 150,000 women served with the WACs. Applicants had to be US citizens between the ages of 21 and 45 with no dependents. WACs served in a number of critical roles, including parachute riggers, mechanics, photographers, stenographers, file clerks, radio operators, and bomb site maintenance specialists. (Author's collection.)

```
           WE'RE THE WACS OF CAMP
                 CROWDER

        Tune:  Original

        We're the Wacs of Camp Crowder
        And we're mighty proud to
             know we're stationed here
        We've a job to do
        We'll see it through
That's what any Wac would do
We're the girls with the army
We are motor corps, dispatchers, typists too
We can't shoot a gun
Or fight the foe
But there's plenty we can do.
We're here to help our fighting men
We'll do every thing we can
We'll stand by the army's fighting men
And "Colonel T's" our man
We're the Wacs from Camp Crowder
And we want you to understand
That we're here until the victory
So give the Crowder Wacs a hand.
```

According to the Center of Military History for the US Army, "The Regional Hospital at Camp Crowder, Missouri, found the services of the WAC so useful that a course was initiated to train Medical Secretaries. It [was] estimated that one doctor and one Medical Secretary can do the work of two doctors." Pictured is a page from a songbook issued to the WACs stationed at Camp Crowder; this specific book belonged to Pfc. Ruby E. Reed and featured the song "We're the WACS of Camp Crowder." (Author's collection.)

91

To My Mother on Her Day

CAMP
CROWDER
MISSOURI

A Day of Loving Memories
And Comfort Rare and True
Because I Have
a Mother Dear
And Because that Mother is YOU

From Your Son in the Service

With Love
Andy

Though far removed from many of the comforts they enjoyed prior to entering the US Army, soldiers undergoing training while stationed at Camp Crowder were able to purchase small cards such as this at one of the 22 post exchanges to send home on Mother's Day to remind their mothers they remained in their thoughts. (Author's collection.)

More Joy for Dad.....

Camp
Crowder,
Missouri

You stand out as the finest
That any Dad could be
And I am grateful
That you belong to me

From Your Son in the Service

Just as the daily rigors of Army life during World War II did not cast a shadow over the memories of a mother, fathers of soldiers who were undergoing training at Camp Crowder were often honored and remembered on Father's Day and other special occasions with commemorative cards purchased and mailed home by their sons. (Author's collection.)

Soldiers in training at the Central Signal Corps Replacement Training Center often learned duties not directly related to communications, which included assignment to chauffeur's training to operate the vehicles used to transport the radio and communications equipment. This was the study guide issued to students undergoing chauffeur's training in 1942, which covered a range of subjects including driver records, reports, hand signals, rules of the road, and extinguishing vehicle fires. (Author's collection.)

This map, included in a booklet provided to soldiers in chauffeur's training at Camp Crowder, shows where the headquarters for the Central Signal Corps Replacement Training Center was located on Laclede Avenue. The former headquarters location is now part of the Crowder College campus, a section of which is home to the Missouri Alternative and Renewable Energy Technology Center. (Courtesy of Museum of Missouri Military History.)

Recruits and draftees arriving at the camp for training were issued a copy of a booklet such as this when assigned to the Basic and Specialist Unit Command. *Basic Notes* provided the trainees with an overview of camp life, exhibited many of the proficiencies they would learn in basic and advance training, and noted the four Signal Corps training regiments—the Sixth, Seventh, Eighth, and Ninth Regimental Training Regiments—and the areas they encompassed. (Courtesy of Museum of Military History.)

During World War II, the post exchanges on Camp Crowder sold several types of notepads with letterhead featuring the insignia of the organization for which a majority of the recruits were training—the Signal Corps. The insignia features crossed red and white wigwag flags with a flaming torch in the center. (Author's collection.)

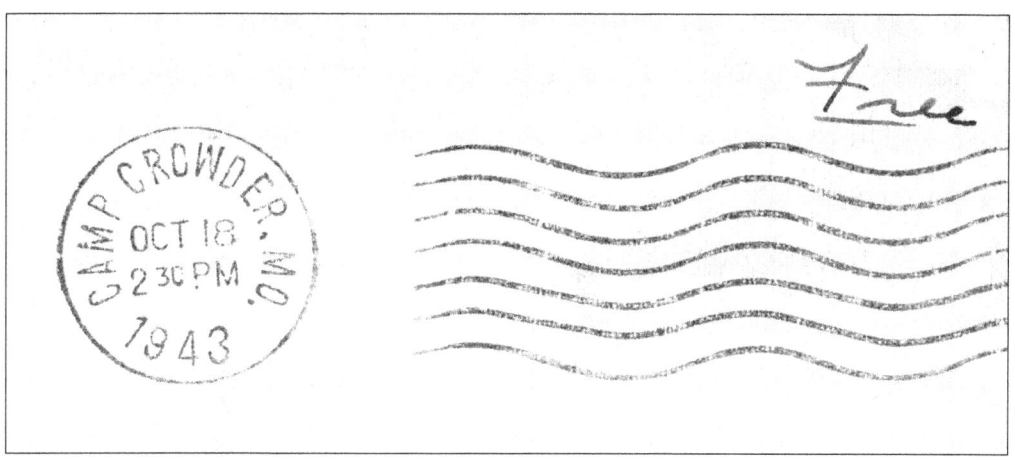

Camp Crowder had a central post office located near the main entrance of the camp, in addition to several branch offices. All of the postal facilities handled the sale of stamps, money orders, and war stamps and bonds. Pictured is a detail from an envelope that was mailed from the camp in 1943, which shows that service members on active duty during the war were granted free postage on letters; however, the free mailing privileges did not apply to packages or air mail. (Author's collection.)

This "Class B" pass was issued to soldiers stationed at Camp Crowder during the latter part of World War II. Such a pass authorized the soldier "to be absent from his station from Reveille until Taps on Sundays and holidays and after Retreat until Taps on week days," as noted on the back of the pass. It was only valid for travel within a 50-mile radius of the camp. (Author's collection.)

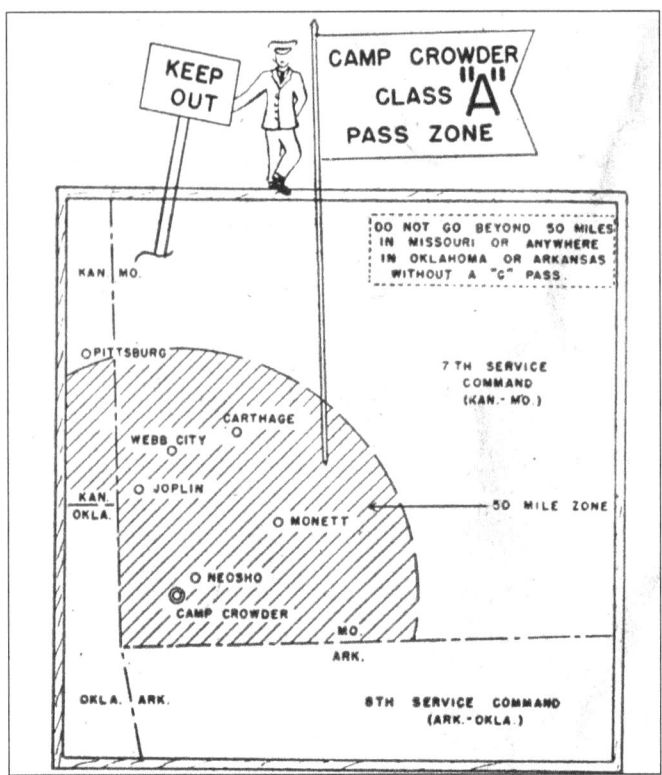

Soldiers with a "Class A" pass at Camp Crowder were given this map to show the areas where they were allowed to travel in their off-duty time. If bus service was not available to a certain location in the authorized area or the lines were too long, service members could catch a taxi from the Field House, where several taxi companies maintained stands. (Author's collection.)

Companies throughout the United States manufactured many types of memorabilia specific to Camp Crowder, which could be purchased by soldiers at the various post exchanges. Pictured here is the cover for a book of matches produced by the Diamond Match Company of New York City and sold at the camp. (Author's collection.)

In March 1942, the Army Service Forces were established as part of a sweeping reorganization to bring together five different components of the US Army. During the war, there were nine service commands, with Camp Crowder falling under the authority of the 7th Service Command, which had headquarters in Omaha, Nebraska. Pictured is the patch of the 7th Service Command worn on the uniforms of many soldiers on Camp Crowder during World War II. (Author's collection)

Many years ago, this detailed concrete representation of the 7th Service Command patch was discovered during some excavation work on Camp Crowder. The large symbol was eventually moved by the Missouri National Guard and placed on display in front of the current headquarters building on the post. (Author's collection.)

There were scores of patriotic envelopes available for purchase to demonstrate support for the war effort during World War II. This particular cover was purchased and mailed on August 23, 1943, by Pfc. Glen Stith from the post office at Camp Crowder under the free mailing privileges granted to service members during the war. (Author's collection.)

This booklet was printed as part of the 1943 Christmas celebration of members of Company D, 848th Signal Training Battalion at Camp Crowder. The booklet lists the menu of the Christmas dinner served for the celebration in addition to the personnel assigned to the company. The following month, the entire battalion was moved to Fort Monmouth where companies were divided between two sub camps—Camp Wood and Camp Edison. (Author's collection.)

This small booklet listing a dinner menu was printed for members of Company A, 840th Signal Training Battalion for their 1943 Thanksgiving celebration. In January 1944, the battalion—comprised of 20 training companies, a headquarters company, and four provisional battalion headquarters teams—was moved from Camp Crowder to Camp Kohler, California. (Author's collection.)

License plate toppers were used on a number of military bases during World War II to denote vehicles owned by enlisted soldiers, officers, or civilian personnel assigned to the base. This particular topper measures 3.5 by 6.5 inches and was issued to an enlisted soldier assigned to Camp Crowder in 1942. The toppers were often much smaller than standard plates due to the shortage of metal during the war. (Author's collection.)

Coupons such as these were issued to customers of the post exchanges at Camp Crowder who purchased bottled products such as soda. The coupon indicates the individual had paid the container deposit, which encouraged the recycling of bottles, since the 3¢ deposit would be returned to the customer once the bottle was brought back to the post exchange. (Courtesy of Museum of Missouri Military History.)

By all appearances, this matchbook produced for Camp Crowder by the Universal Match Corporation in St. Louis might seem a standard matchbook cover; however, it doubled as a postcard. Once the matches were used, the matchbook could be flattened to serve as a divided back postcard that could be mailed for a penny. (Author's collection.)

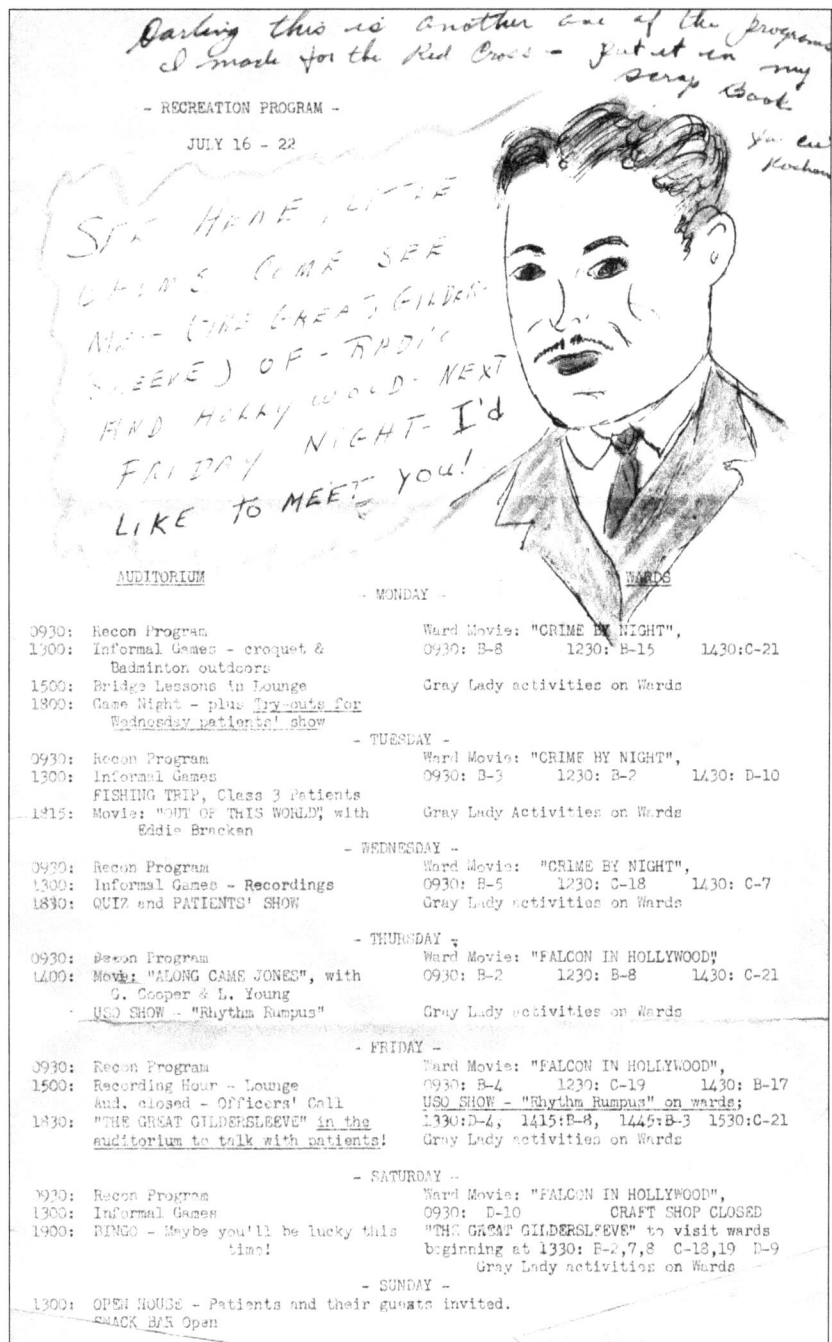

Soldiers in the Reconditioning Section at the camp hospital also underwent Educational Reconditioning to help enable them to either return to duty or to be in the best physical and mental condition if discharged. This program provided recovering soldiers such opportunities as working in the photo laboratory, with the hospital newspaper, in the art studio, or with the arts and craft workshop. This handbill, highlighting one week of recreational events at the post hospital, was created in the summer of 1945 by a soldier in the Educational Reconditioning program. (Author's collection.)

```
                              CTC-41-8
                HAND RECEIPT

            Co "A" 35th Sig Tng Bn
            Camp Crowder, Missouri

       Name    SHEA            WALTER
       (Print) Last            First

       ASN   33939472   BARRACKS  1227

            I certify that I have this date
       received from Co "A" 35th Sig Tng Bn
       the following listed items:

            Date    May 3, 1945

       1    Blankets, wool, OD
       1    Comforter
       1    Pillowcase
       1    Cover, mattress
       1    Mattress
       1    Pillow
       1    Cot, steel
       1    Locker, trunk
       ___  _____
       ___  _____
       ___  _____

       W.S.  EM Initials
```

When Pvt. Walter D. Shea arrived for training with Company A, 35th Signal Training Battalion at Camp Crowder in May 1945, he was given this hand receipt to denote the items he was issued before reporting to the company barracks. Shea was inducted into the US Army in New Cumberland, Pennsylvania, on May 16, 1944. The World War II veteran passed away on December 12, 1979, and was laid to rest in Camden, New Jersey. (Author's collection.)

Seven
THE SURROUNDING COMMUNITIES

One of the primary forms of communication used by soldiers in training at Camp Crowder during World War II was postcards. This postcard from the 1940s is among the type that were available for purchase at the post exchanges on Camp Crowder. Located near Neosho, Missouri, the site for the camp was selected because of its proximity to water, two major railroads, and major highways (US 71 running north-south and US 60 and Route 66 running east-west). (Author's collection.)

The Big Spring Inn in downtown Neosho was a popular place to stay for people traveling to Neosho or simply passing through the area. Many individuals involved in the construction and development of Camp Crowder stayed at the inn while the families and loved ones of soldiers assigned to the post would become a large part of its clientele during the war years. The inn burned down in November 1966 and was not rebuilt. (Author's collection.)

The Sale-Bowman Hospital, located on the northwest corner of South Jefferson and Main Streets in Neosho, became an important provider of medical care in the early days of Camp Crowder. Prior to the opening of the hospital at Camp Crowder in mid-January 1942, Sale-Bowman Hospital (now Freeman Neosho Hospital), along with other area facilities, helped provide emergency medical care to workers injured at the camp in addition to soldiers who became ill. (Author's collection.)

Home to a beautiful garden, wading pool, and trout and koi pond, Big Spring Park was founded in 1903 to serve the community of Neosho. Located at 309 West Spring Street, the park is fed by a spring historically known as Clark Spring and became a popular site for families to spend time visiting with their loved ones stationed at Camp Crowder. (Author's collection.)

Seven miles from Camp Crowder, Sagamount Inn was a popular summer destination and became renowned not only for Sunday dinners, but also for its spring-fed swimming pools and miniature golf course. The inn was cooled in the summer and heated in the winter from a shaft drilled into the cave beneath. Rooms rented for $6 a week during World War II. (Author's collection.)

This postcard from the early 1940s features the Neosho National Fish Hatchery. It became the government's first fish hatchery in 1888 because of its 60-degree springs and rail service, which allowed for the movement of fish across the Midwest. During the latter part of World War II, soldiers from Camp Crowder were allowed to fish at the hatchery as long as they purchased the appropriate state fishing license. (Author's collection.)

This postcard from the early 1940s shows a section of the Elk River, often referred to locally as the Cowskin River, located near Camp Crowder. Soldiers on leave from the camp would often rent motorboats on the river. However, tragedy struck in June 1943 when 21-year-old Cpl. Virgil H. Deal, a soldier stationed at Crowder, was killed during a boating accident. His body was returned to his native Montana for burial. (Author's collection.)

With a population of more than 37,000 during World War II, Joplin, little more than 20 miles from the camp, offered greater opportunities for entertainment and nightlife than nearby Neosho. During the war, military equipment from Camp Crowder would on occasion be displayed on the streets of downtown Joplin as part of US Army recruiting initiatives. (Author's collection.)

The interior of the USO Club in Joplin is pictured in this postcard from the 1940s. Located at 310 Wall Street, the club hosted a number of events for service members and their guests, including dinners, dances, movies, and sporting events. Since the clubs, like the military, were often segregated, a USO Club for black soldiers was opened on the second floor of a building at 221 Main Street on February 6, 1944. (Author's collection.)

Main Street in Joplin became a regular haunt for off-duty soldiers at Camp Crowder as they visited the various businesses, eating establishments, and lounges in an effort to escape—if only for a little while—the daily rigors of Army life. The street also served as the main route for Armed Forces Day Parades, which in the early 1950s included music from Camp Crowder's 317th Army Band. (Courtesy of Missouri State Archives.)

Col. Dennis E. McCunniff assumed command of Camp Crowder in April 1946. On May 2, 1946, Colonel McCunniff, in an effort to show his appreciation to the community for their support of the camp, hosted a group of 14 civic leaders from Neosho for a dinner at the Officer's Club on Camp Crowder. Colonel McCunniff is pictured at the far end of the table with Neosho mayor Russell A. Johnson. (Courtesy of Missouri State Archives.)

This postcard from 1944 shows the interior of the Army and Navy Masonic Center at 105 South Washington Street in Neosho. The center opened on May 9, 1942, in a building once occupied by a Firestone tire store. It not only provided services in support of service members in the area, but also had a powder room and restroom for mothers, wives, and girlfriends of soldiers. As of December 31, 1942, it was one of three such centers in Missouri and more than 40 nationwide made possible by the Masonic Service Association. (Author's collection.)

Located nearly 30 miles north of Camp Crowder, the community of Carthage, Missouri, provided significant support to the soldiers at the nearby camp by remodeling its former Elks Club facility into a USO club during the war. Additionally, baseball teams from Camp Crowder would frequently engage in recreational games against many local teams; some of these ball games were held at Carthage Municipal Park. (Author's collection.)

The Newton County Courthouse in Neosho was built of Carthage stone in 1936 and occupies the center of the public square. In 1941, the auditorium of the new courthouse was used to hold meetings attended by farmers of Newton and McDonald Counties who were likely to be relocated because of the construction of Camp Crowder. Later in the war, it also played host to naturalization ceremonies for men from many different countries who took their oath of citizenship while serving in uniform. (Author's collection.)

The Neosho Auditorium and City Hall was built at a cost of $90,000 and dedicated on September 28, 1938. During World War II, the auditorium was used for many patriotic events, including shows to encourage the purchase of war bonds. In May 1943, one such show featured local talent and was titled *Cavalcade of an American*—a musical written by a soldier of the 804th Signal Training Regiment that featured soldiers of Camp Crowder in the cast. (Author's collection.)

Churches near Camp Crowder not only served as spiritual homes for many of the soldiers during their temporary assignments at the post, but they also became marriage ceremony sites for those who were engaged to women from the local community. The First Methodist Church of Joplin hosted one such couple on June 12, 1945, when Cpl. William T. Murray of San Jacinto, California, who was stationed at Camp Crowder, wed Pauline Gilbreath of Joplin. (Author's collection.)

Eight
Camp Crowder after World War II

Remnants of an area once used by the Wire Training Section at Camp Crowder are still visible near the junction of Benton Avenue and Lewis Drive, which is now property owned by Crowder College. Many Signal Corps linemen at the post received instruction under the guidance of Lt. Clinton Green, who prior to the war was an employee of the Iowa-Illinois Telephone Company and the Iowa Southern Utilities Company. (Author's collection.)

The Officer's Club on Camp Crowder was available for off-duty recreational purposes for commissioned officers, warrant officers, and nurses of the garrison during World War II. Not only were meals served at the club, but there were courts for tennis and badminton in addition to ping-pong, pool, and billiards. The remains of the club are now on private property south of Route D/Lyon Drive, east of the former Lyon Gate entrance. (Author's collection.)

Although there were hundreds of buildings erected on Camp Crowder during its early years, few original structures remain. Among them are these buildings on Thain Street. They are the property of Crowder College; however, the Missouri National Guard continues to utilize and maintain the facilities. (Author's collection.)

The deactivation of Camp Crowder was announced in March 1946, and the post was declared surplus on January 13, 1947. The following year, 1,004 buildings on the original post were sold and moved. One of the buildings surviving the sale is this mess hall on Thain Street, which sees continued use as a dining facility by the Missouri National Guard. (Author's collection.)

Camp Crowder became the site of a disciplinary barracks in 1953 and was designated a permanent fort in 1955. This ended in 1958 when it was placed in standby status; a few years later, it was inactivated and the property sold as surplus. The Missouri National Guard retained 4,358 acres of what was originally nearly 43,000 acres for use as a training site and has in recent years constructed newer barracks such as these to house troops staying at the camp for training exercises. (Author's collection.)

The interior of the barracks buildings utilized by the Missouri National Guard maintain much of their World War II–era charm, with wooden floors and bunks lining the outer walls. Some of the original buildings such as this, which survived the sale of structures in 1948, were utilized when the camp was reactivated on May 30, 1951, to serve as a reception and processing center for the Korean War. (Author's collection.)

What remains of the once expansive parade grounds on Camp Crowder is seen here from Clark Drive looking northwest. The property is now owned by Crowder College and much of it paved to provide a training area for the college's program to train tractor-trailer operators. During World War II, the scene would have featured an open grassy area with buildings along the perimeter that included post exchanges, chapels, and the Sergeants' Club. (Author's collection.)

The main entrance to Camp Crowder is now located on Ray A. Carver Avenue, which in years past was named Linn Avenue. The avenue was renamed in 1989 to honor the late Ray Allen Carver of Pierce City, Missouri—a 32-year veteran of the Missouri National Guard who earned a Bronze Star while serving with the US Army in World War II. (Author's collection.)

Ray A. Carver is pictured in a 2008 photograph taken for the dedication of the Ray A. Carver Building in Pierce City, which was previously the armory for the Missouri National Guard's 203rd Engineer Battalion. Carver began his career as a unit administrator for the Missouri National Guard in 1952 and served in that capacity until 1974. The veteran then went on to serve in a civilian capacity as post engineer for Camp Crowder from 1974 until 1988. He passed away in 2012. (Courtesy of Larry Carver.)

Remnants of the days of segregation in the military can still be seen on Camp Crowder in the form of these concrete coal bunkers in an area once referred to as "Shanty Town." These foundations for the bunkers are in a section of the camp once used to house African American soldiers during the war, which were poor facilities that included outdoor latrines. Many of the soldiers housed in this area of the camp belonged to the all–African American 43rd Signal Construction Battalion activated at Camp Crowder in February 1944. (Author's collection.)

The 43rd Signal Construction Battalion was redesignated the 43rd Heavy Construction Battalion in March 1944 and went on to serve in several major campaigns during World War II before being deactivated in Germany in May 1946. Foundations from the buildings that once housed the all–African American group in the segregated area of Camp Crowder serve as a lasting testament to the battalion's wartime service on property now owned by the Missouri National Guard. (Author's collection.)

When turning off Highway 71 onto Route D, also known as Lyon Drive, motorists have this view of a four-lane highway, looking east. This highway once led to a sprawling military post nearly 43,000 acres in size and with a peak population of more than 40,000 during World War II. Today, Route D intersects Doniphan Drive near the entrance to Crowder College. (Author's collection.)

The four-lane road that served as the main entrance to Camp Crowder, Lyon Drive, passed under Kansas City Southern Railroad tracks. The eastern side of the underpass still contains a painted statement, much of which is still visible. Hailing from the camp's World War II and Korean War retention efforts, it reads, "It adds up! Be Smart! Stay In! RE-ENLIST!" (Author's collection.)

The weapons ranges at Camp Crowder are located along Hughes Road on property that was retained by the Missouri National Guard and used for small arms ranges in the early days of the post. The National Guard has not only updated the ranges, but has added areas where soldiers can operate and qualify on crew-served weapons. Pictured is the range tower erected at the entrance of the M-16 rifle range. (Author's collection.)

On the backside of the rifle range is this concrete wall from which targets were manually lifted for range firing during World War II; the Missouri National Guard has since automated the targets. Throughout the years, a tradition emerged in which soldiers training at the camp, in addition to civilian visitors, signed their names on the wall. (Author's collection.)

One name found scribbled among the thousands on the concrete wall behind the rifle range on Camp Crowder is that of actor, comedian, and World War II veteran Dick Van Dyke, who according to his signature visited the post on April 13, 1954. Years later, Van Dyke's character in *The Dick Van Dyke Show*, Rob Petrie, would reference his service at Camp Crowder during World War II, based upon the experiences of producer Carl Reiner. (Author's collection.)

During World War II, the intersection of Laclede Avenue and Doniphan Drive was the southwest corner of the parade ground on Camp Crowder, with the post headquarters located nearby. Crowder College was founded in 1963 and the following year began operations in buildings that were once part of Camp Crowder. The intersection now serves as the main entrance to the college campus. (Author's collection.)

Along Laclede Avenue, which now serves as the main entrance to Crowder College, remains evidence of the layout of Camp Crowder during World War II. The lengthy drainage ditch along the roadway was constructed from native stone by POW labor. The ditch runs along part of what was once the southeastern edge of the camp's parade field. (Author's collection.)

The remnants of this World War II–era incinerator complex remain on the northern section of Camp Crowder in an area controlled by the Missouri National Guard. Although the complex is essentially abandoned, during both World War II and the Korean War, many types of solid waste would have been disposed of in the incinerator. (Author's collection.)

In 1956, the US Air Force, on property that was once part of Camp Crowder, broke ground for a plant that would later produce and test engines for the Redstone, Atlas, Thor, and Jupiter rockets as well as produce components for the Saturn. The Air Force assigned the plant to Rocketdyne—a division of North American Aviation Inc.—which delivered its first engine to the Air Force in February 1958. Officially known as Air Force Plant No. 65, Rocketdyne ceased operations at the plant in 1968, and the facility was later used by companies for component overhaul and jet engine turbine repair. The plant has since closed. (Author's collection.)

There are two engine test stands located in an area of Camp Crowder that was known as the Engine Test Area. US Air Force contractors would suspend rocket engines in this test stand to measure performance while employees were protected in nearby bunkers equipped with blast deflectors. Pictured is the north Engine Test Area as it appears today. (Author's collection.)

The rocket testing process created significant quantities of waste fuels and lubricants, primarily trichloroethylene. When the performance tests on the engines and components were completed, they were drained of their fuel into these concrete drainage ditches that flowed to hazardous waste pits and storage lagoons. The process led to water and soil contamination in the area and has in recent years required cleanup and mitigation, which has been overseen by the US Environmental Protection Agency and the Missouri Department of Natural Resources. (Author's collection.)

US Air Force contractors employed in testing various rocket engines utilized two bunkers in a service and components area that were connected to the ETA through underground tunnels. One of these bunkers, pictured here, is currently used by the Missouri National Guard as a protective shelter during threatening weather. (Author's collection.)

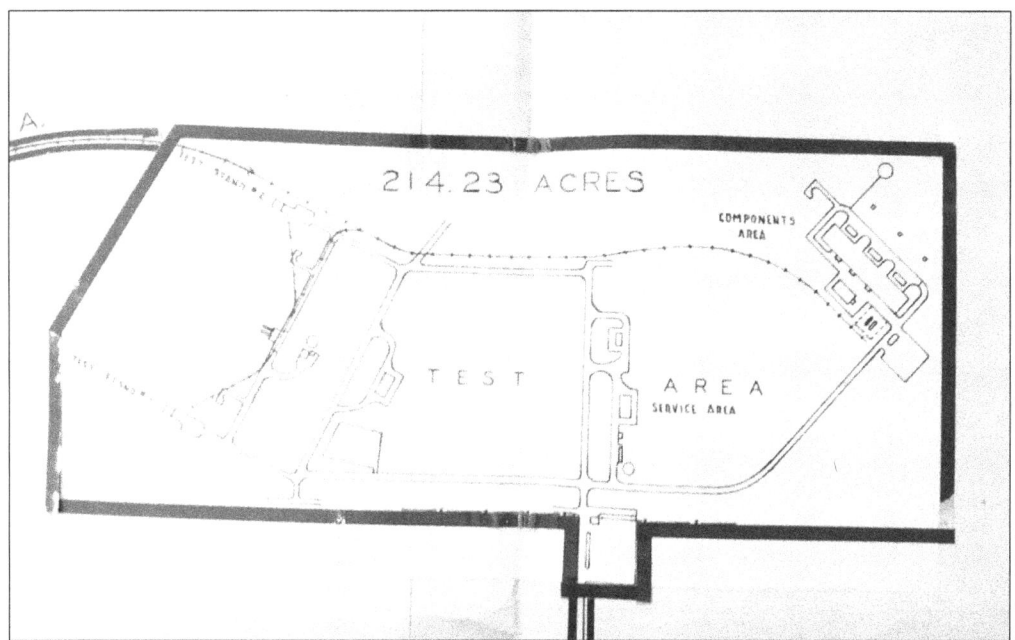

This survey from July 1965 shows the layout of the 214.23 acres used by US Air Force contractors as a test area for engines of various rockets during the Cold War. In addition to the two stands where tests were performed, the area was comprised of a service area to perform maintenance on the engines and a components area where testing was conducted on specific components used in the construction of the engines. (Courtesy of Museum of Missouri Military History.)

Many of the originally named streets are still in existence on Camp Crowder, at Crowder College, and throughout the local community. Thain Street, which is located along property owned by Crowder College, was named in recognition of the late John Ewart Thain (1870–1961), a Scottish immigrant who later settled in the Neosho area and whose property was consumed in the construction of Camp Crowder. (Author's collection.)

Bibliography

"A Real War Service by Masonic Service Center." *Neosho Daily News*. December 31, 1942.

"Crowder Reconditioning Section Has 'Open House.'" *Joplin Globe*. July 18, 1944.

"Eddie Bracken Dies at 87; Acted in Sturges Comedies." *The New York Times*. November 16, 2002.

"Expect Troops to Neosho by Christmas." *Macon Chronicle-Herald*. October 20, 1941.

Fiedler, David. *The Enemy Among Us: POWs in Missouri During World War II*. St. Louis, MO: Missouri Historical Society Press, 2003.

"Finds WACs on Duty at Camp Crowder." *Des Moines Register*. July 9, 1944.

"Gen. Ingles Arrives to Inspect Crowder." *Joplin Globe*. August 25, 1944.

Hively, Kay. *Red Hot and Dusty: Tales of Camp Crowder*. Cassville, MO: Litho Printers, 1983.

"Instruction in Line Work Given by Lt. C. Green." *Muscatine Journal*. October 26, 1944.

"It All Began With a Lost Piece of Artwork." *Neosho Daily News*. April 15, 2009.

Johnson, Danny. "Camp Enoch H. Crowder, Missouri." Army Historical Foundation, January 28, 2015.

"Open House at Camp Crowder." *Neosho Daily News*. March 8, 1945.

"Safety Record Established at Camp Crowder." *Neosho Daily News*. January 7, 1942.

"Water Warning to Neosho Residents." *Neosho Daily News*. May 19, 1943.

Visit us at
arcadiapublishing.com

www.ingramcontent.com/pod-product-compliance
Lightning Source LLC
Chambersburg PA
CBHW060937170426
43194CB00027B/2979